S0-BFE-410

THE LAW (IN PLAIN ENGLISH)®

FOR SMALL BUSINESSES

Other books by Leonard D. DuBoff

Madrona Publishers' Law (in Plain English)® Series

  The Law (in Plain English)® for Craftspeople

  Business Forms and Contracts (in Plain English)® for Craftspeople

  The Law (in Plain English)® for Writers

The Deskbook of Art Law and 1984 Supplement

The Book Publishers' Legal Guide

Art Law in a Nutshell

Law and the Visual Arts

Art Law, Domestic and International

THE LAW
(IN PLAIN ENGLISH)®
FOR SMALL BUSINESSES

Leonard D. DuBoff

Madrona Publishers   Seattle

To Mary Ann Crawford DuBoff, my partner in life and in law

Copyright © 1987 by Leonard D. DuBoff
All Rights Reserved
Printed in the United States of America

Published by
Madrona Publishers
P. O. Box 22667
Seattle, WA 98122

10 9 8 7 6 5 4 3 2 1

Library of Congress Cataloging-in-Publication Data

DuBoff, Leonard D.
   The law (in plain English) for small businesses.

   Includes index.
   1. Business law--United States.   I. Title.
KF889.6.D83   1987   346.73'07   87-14887
                          347.3067
ISBN 0-88089-023-1 (pbk.)

Contents

Foreword

Business life is more complex than ever. Small business operates in an environment of rapid change: new products, technology, suppliers, customers. Changes in law also have altered the working environment of the small-business owner. In this eminently sensible and usable book, Leonard D. DuBoff provides essential information about organizing a business, borrowing money, stock issues, contracts, consignment, collections, franchises, marketing, patents, copyrights, licenses, consumer protection, employee relations. He concludes with advice on how, if necessary, to choose an attorney or accountant. The book is clearly written, and it should be kept close at hand for anyone involved in a small business.

William H. Becker

Professor of History and Business Administration
The George Washington University

General Editor
The Encyclopedia of American Business History and Biography

Preface

For years, law students and business clients have asked me to recommend a book which could provide a general business background for a non-lawyer. After reviewing the material available on the market, I was unable to find any book which satisfied this requirement. My mission, therefore, in writing this was to fill that niche and provide a book for non-lawyers which covers some fundamental business concepts. Each of the subjects discussed here could be the subject of a complete law school course and all have been addressed in legal treatises. This is not intended as a substitute for the numerous legal tomes available. Readers who are interested in learning more about particular subjects should browse through the host of books available in a law library.

Our legal system is so complex, and evolving so rapidly, that even trained experts are hard pressed to keep up with new developments. Unfortunately, it is quite common for the owner of a small business to become embroiled in a complex legal problem before he or she is able to recognize the difficulty. One of my goals in preparing this book was to enable the reader to identify problem areas and seek the aid of a professional when necessary—or, preferably, before it becomes necessary.

This book is not intended to be a substitute for the advice of a professional; rather, it is designed to sensitize you to the issues which may require the aid of a skilled attorney or other expert. It is my sincere hope that this book will, like its three predecessors in the (In Plain English)® series, be practical, useful, and readable.

When I commenced working on this, I once again enlisted the aid of friends, colleagues, and former students. I am extremely indebted to a host of individuals for their comments, suggestions, and assistance with the myriad tasks which are necessary when preparing a manuscript for publication.

It may be impossible to identify all of those who have contributed in some way to the quality of this work. Still, there are some who deserve special mention. I would like to express my appreciation to all of my friends and former students and in particular acknowledge the fine work of: Alice Bennison, JD, Lewis and Clark, 1987; Georgene Inaba, JD, Lewis and Clark, 1985; Nancy Walseth, JD, Lewis and Clark, 1978; Jason Cappello, JD, Lewis and Clark, 1984; James Losk, JD, Lewis and Clark, 1987; Melody Ghormley, paralegal with the law firm of Joseph, Babener & Carpenter; and Michelle Gold, of the Lewis and Clark Law School.

Two of my colleagues at the Northwestern School of Law of Lewis and Clark College, Larry Brown and Jack Bogdanski, both tax experts, have been kind enough to critique and provide many useful comments on the chapters dealing with tax and estate planning. Jeffrey Babener of the Portland, Oregon, law firm of Joseph, Babener & Carpenter was kind enough to assist me with the material on writing a business plan, franchising, and multilevel marketing. Many of the ideas expressed in this text on those subjects are based on his more complete and scholarly works.

Lenair Mulford has once again worked her magic with the word processor and managed to convert a collection of notes, interlineations, scraps, and changes into a publishable manuscript. Thanks must also go to my editor, Sara Levant, managing editor at Madrona Publishers, for her sharp attention to the details.

Finally, I would like to express my sincere appreciation for the understanding, support, and assistance of my wife, Mary Ann Crawford DuBoff, and my children, Colleen Rose DuBoff, Robert Courtney DuBoff, and Sabrina Ashley DuBoff. Without their support, this book could not have become a reality.

THE LAW (IN PLAIN ENGLISH)®

FOR SMALL BUSINESSES

1

Organizing Your Business

Everyone in business knows that survival requires careful financial planning. Yet few fully realize the importance of selecting the best *form* for the business. Small businesses have little need for the sophisticated organizational structures utilized in industry, but since all entrepreneurs must pay taxes, obtain loans, and expose themselves to potential liability with every sale they make, it only makes sense to structure one's business so as to minimize these concerns.

Every business has an organizational form best suited to it. When I counsel people on organizing their businesses, I usually adopt a two-step approach. First, we discuss various aspects of taxes and liability in order to decide which of the basic forms is best. There are only a handful of basic forms: the *sole proprietorship*, the *partnership*, the *corporation*, and a few hybrids. Then, once we have decided which of these is appropriate, we go into the organizational details such as partnership agreements or corporate bylaws. These documents define the day-to-day operations of a business and therefore must be tailored to individual situations.

What I offer here is an explanation of the features of these kinds of organization, including their advantages and disadvantages. This should give you some idea of which form might be best for you.

I will discuss potential problems but, since I cannot go into a full discussion of the more intricate details, you should consult an attorney before deciding to adopt any particular structure. My purpose here is to facilitate your communication with your lawyer and to enable you to better understand the choices offered.

The American Dream: Sole Proprietorship

The technical name *sole proprietorship* may be unfamiliar to you, but chances are you are operating under this form now. The sole proprietorship is an unincorporated business owned by one person. Though not peculiar to the United States, it was, and still is, the backbone of the American dream, to the extent that personal freedom follows economic freedom. As a form of business it is elegant in its simplicity. All it requires is a little money and work. Legal requirements are few and simple. In most localities, you must obtain a business license from the city or county for a small fee. If you wish to operate the business under a name other than your own, the name must be registered with the state and, in some cases, the county in which you are doing business. With these details taken care of, you are in business.

Disadvantages of Sole Proprietorship

There are many financial risks involved in operating your business as a sole proprietor. If you recognize any of these dangers as a real threat, you probably should consider an alternative form of organization.

If you are the sole proprietor of a business venture, the property you personally own is at stake. In other words, if for any reason you owe more than the dollar value of your business, your creditors can force a sale of most of your property to satisfy the debt.

For many risks, insurance is available which will shift the loss from you to an insurance company, but there are some risks for which insurance is simply not available. For instance, insurance is not generally available to protect against a large rise in the cost, or sudden unavailability, of supplies or raw materials. In addition, the cost of product-liability insurance has become so high that, as a practical matter, it is unavailable to most businesses. Even when procured, every insurance policy has a limited, strictly defined scope of coverage. These liability risks, as well as many other uncertain economic factors, can drive a small business into bankruptcy, and that, in turn, could force you into personal bankruptcy if you are the sole proprietor.

Taxes for the Sole Proprietor

The sole proprietor is taxed on all profits of the business and may deduct losses. Of course, the rate of taxation will fluctuate with changes in income. A particularly successful year can leave the sole proprietor no better off financially than in the less successful years, due to the higher tax bracket.

Fortunately, there are ways to ease this tax burden. For instance, you can establish an approved IRA or pension plan, deducting a specified amount of your net income for placement into the pension plan, or into an interest-bearing account, or into approved government securities or mutual funds to be withdrawn later when you are in a lower tax bracket. There are severe restrictions, however, on withdrawal of this money prior to retirement age.

For further information on tax planning devices, you should contact your local IRS office and ask for free pamphlets. Or you might wish to use the services of an accountant experienced in dealing with business-tax planning.

Partnership

A *partnership* is defined by most state laws as an association of two or more persons to conduct, as co-owners, a business for profit. No formalities are required. In fact, in some cases people have been held to be partners even though they never had any intention of forming a partnership. For example, if you lend a friend some money to start a business and the friend agrees to pay you a certain percentage of whatever profit is made, you may be your friend's partner in the eyes of the law even though you take no part in running the business. This is important because each partner is subject to unlimited personal liability for the debts of the partnership. Also, each partner is liable for the negligence of another partner and of the partnership's employees when a negligent act occurs in the usual course of business. In effect, each partner is considered an employee of the partnership.

This means that if you are getting involved in a partnership, you should be especially cautious in two areas. First, since the involvement of a partner increases your potential liability, you should choose a responsible partner. Second, the partnership should be adequately insured to protect both the assets of the partnership and the personal assets of each partner.

As I have already mentioned, no formalities are required to create a partnership. If the partners do not have a formal agreement defining the terms of the partnership—such as control of the partnership or the distribution of profits—state law will determine the terms. State laws are based on the fundamental characteristics of the typical partnership as it has existed throughout the ages and are therefore thought to correspond to the reasonable expectations of the partners. The most important of these legally presumed characteristics are:

1. No one can become a member of a partnership without the unanimous consent of all partners,
2. All members have an equal vote in the management of the partnership regardless of the size of their interest in it,
3. All partners share equally in the profits and losses of the partnership no matter how much capital they have contributed,
4. A simple majority vote is required for decisions in the ordinary course of business, and a unanimous vote is required to change the fundamental character of the business, and
5. A partnership is terminable at will by any partner; a partner can withdraw from the partnership at any time, and this withdrawal will cause a dissolution of the partnership.

Most state laws contain a provision that allows the partners to make their own agreements regarding the management structure and division of profits that best suits the needs of the individual partners.

Major Items of Agreement

Some of the major considerations in preparing a partnership agreement include the name of the partnership, a description of the business, contributions of capital by the partners, duration of the partnership, distribution of profits, management responsibilities, duties of partners, prohibited acts, and provisions for the dissolution of the partnership.

As you can see, a comprehensive partnership agreement is no simple matter. It is, in fact, essential for potential partners to devote some time to preparation of an agreement and to enlist the services of a business lawyer. The expense of a lawyer to help you put together an agreement suited to the needs of your partnership is well justified by the amount of money you will save in the smooth organization, operation, and, when necessary, final dissolution of the partnership.

The economic advantages of doing business in a partnership are the pooling of capital, collaboration, easier access to credit because of the collective credit rating, and a potentially more efficient allocation of labor and resources. A major disadvantage is that each partner is fully and personally liable for all the debts of the partnership, even if not personally involved in incurring those debts.

Taxes

A partnership does not possess any special tax advantages over a sole proprietorship. As a partner you will pay tax on your share of the profits whether they are distributed to you or not. You will also be entitled to the same proportion of the partnership deductions and credits. The partnership must file with the IRS an annual information return known as a K-1 form, against which the IRS can check the individual returns filed by the partners.

The Limited Partnership

The *limited partnership* is a hybrid containing elements of both the partnership and corporation. A limited partnership may be formed when one or more parties wishes to invest in a business and, in return, share in its profits, but does not wish to share in any respect in the control of the partnership.

In effect the limited partner is very much like an investor who buys a few shares of stock. Because of the limited partner's passive role, the law limits his or her liability only to the amount invested. In order to establish a limited partnership it is necessary to have one or more general partners to run the business, and one or more limited partners who play a passive role. A general partner will have the same potential liability, duties, and authority as a member of a regular partnership.

In order to form a limited partnership, you must file a document with the proper state office. If the document is not filed or is improperly filed, the limited partner could be treated as a general partner. The limited partner *must* refrain from trying to influence the day-to-day operation of the partnership. Otherwise, the limited partner might be found to be actively participating in the business, and thereby held to be a general partner with unlimited personal liability.

This limited partnership might be appropriate if you need economic backing and wish to reward your sponsor with a share of your profits from the sale of your work without exposing the backer to personal liability. A limited partnership can be used to attract investment when credit is hard to get or is too expensive. In return for investing, the limited partner receives a designated share of the profits. This may be an attractive way to fund your business since the limited partner receives nothing if there are no profits, whereas if you had borrowed money from a creditor, that person could sue if you failed to repay.

Another use of the limited partnership is to facilitate reorganization of a general partnership after the death or retirement of a general partner. A partnership, remember, can be terminated when any partner requests it. Although the original partnership is thus technically dissolved when one partner retires, it is not uncommon for the remaining partners to agree to buy out the retiring partner's share—that is, to return that person's capital contribution and keep the business going. However, a practical problem arises if a large cash source is not available, in which case the partners might be forced to liquidate some or all of the partnership's assets to return the capital contribution. If, rather than withdrawing, the retiring partner simply steps into a limited-partner status, he or she can continue to share in profits (which are in some part, at least, the fruits of that partner's past labor), while removing personal assets from the risk of partnership liabilities yet not forcing the other partners immediately to come up with the capital contribution.

The Eight Basics of a Partnership Agreement

The Name of the Partnership

Most partnerships simply use as names the surnames of the major partners. The choice in that case is nothing more than the order of names, which depends on various factors from prestige to the way the names sound. If a name other than the partners' is used, it will be necessary to file the proposed business name with the state. Care should be taken to choose a name which is distinctive and not already in use. If the name is not distinctive, others can copy it; if the name is already in use, you could be liable for trade-name infringement.

A Description of the Business

In describing their business, the partners should agree on the basic scope of the business—its requirements in regard to capital and labor, the parties' individual contributions of capital and labor, and perhaps some plans regarding future growth.

Partnership Capital

After determining how much capital to contribute, the partners must decide when it will be contributed, how to value the property contributed, and whether there is to be a right to contribute more or to withdraw any at a later date.

Duration of the Partnership

Sometimes partnerships are organized for a fixed amount of time or are automatically dissolved on certain conditions such as the completion of a project.

Distribution of Profits

You can make whatever arrangement you want for distribution. Although ordinarily a partner does not receive a salary, it is possible to give an active partner a guaranteed salary in addition to a share of the profits. Since the partnership's profits can be determined only at the close of a business year, ordinarily no distribution is made until that time. However, it is possible to allow the partners a monthly draw of money against their final share of profits. In some cases it may be necessary to allow limited expense accounts for some partners.

Not all of the profits of the partnership need to be distributed at year's end. Some can be retained for expansion, an arrangement that can be provided for in the partnership agreement. Note, though, that whether the profits are distributed or not, all partners must pay tax on their shares. The tax code refers directly to the partnership agreement to determine what that share is, which shows how important a partnership agreement is.

Management

The division of power in the partnership can be made in many ways. All partners can be given an equal voice, or some more than others. A few partners might be allowed to manage the business entirely, the remaining partners being given a vote only on specifically designated areas of concern. Besides voting, three other areas of management should be covered. First is the question of who can sign checks, place orders, or enter into contracts on behalf of the partnership. Under state partnership laws any partner may do these things so long as they are in the usual course of business. But such a broad delegation of authority can lead to confusion, so it might be best to delegate this authority more narrowly.

Second, it is a good idea to determine a regular date for partnership meetings. Third, some consideration should be given to the possibility of a disagreement among the partners that leads to a deadlock. One way to avoid this is to distribute the voting power in such a way as to make a deadlock impossible. However, in a two-person partnership this would mean that one partner would be in absolute control. This might be unacceptable to the other partner. If, instead, the power is divided evenly among an even number of partners, as is often the case, the agreement should stipulate a neutral party or arbitrator who could settle any dispute and thereby avoid a dissolution of the partnership.

Prohibited Acts

By law, each partner owes the partnership certain duties by virtue of being an employee or agent of the partnership. First is the duty of diligence. This means the partner must exercise reasonable care in acting as a partner. Second is a duty of obedience. The partner must obey the rules of the partnership and, most importantly, must not exceed the authority that the partnership has vested in him or her. Finally, there is a duty of loyalty. A partner may not, without approval of the other partners, compete with the partnership in another business. A partner may not seize upon a business opportunity that would be of value to the partnership without first telling the partnership about it and allowing the partnership to pursue it.

A list of acts prohibited to any partner should be made a part of the partnership agreement, elaborating and expanding on these fundamental duties.

Dissolution and Liquidation

A partnership is automatically dissolved upon the death, withdrawal, or expulsion of a partner. Dissolution identifies the legal end of the partnership but need not affect its economic life if the partnership agreement has provided for the continuation of the business after a dissolution. Nonetheless, a dissolution will affect the business because the partner who withdraws or is expelled, or the estate of the deceased partner, will be entitled to a return of the proportionate share of capital that the departing partner contributed. Details such as how this capital will be returned should be decided before dissolution, because at the time of dissolution it may be impossible to negotiate. One method of handling this is to provide for a return of the capital in cash over a period of time. Some provision should be made so the remaining partners will know how much of a departing partner's interest they may purchase.

After a partner leaves, the partnership may need to be reorganized and recapitalized. Again, provision for this should be worked out in advance, if possible. Finally, since it is always possible that the partners will eventually want to liquidate the partnership, it should be decided in advance who will liquidate the assets, which assets will be distributed, and what property will be returned to its original contributor.

What You Don't Want: Unintended Partners

Whether yours is a straightforward partnership or a limited partnership, one arrangement you want to avoid is the unintended partnership. This can occur when you work together with another person and your relationship is not described formally. Thus, if you and another person decide to import, market and sell small electronic appliances from Asia, it is essential for you to spell out in detail the arrangements between you and the other person. If you do not, you could find that the other person is your partner and entitled to half of the income you receive even though the contribution was minimal. You can avoid this by simply hiring the other person or paying that person a percentage of what you are paid, making that person a commissioned employee. Whichever arrangement you choose, you should have a detailed written agreement.

The Corporation

The word "corporation" may call to mind a vision of a large company with hundreds or thousands of employees. In fact, the vast majority of corporations in the United States are small or moderate-size companies. There are advantages and disadvantages to incorporating; if it appears advantageous to incorporate, you will find it can be done with surprising ease and with little expense. However, you will need a lawyer's assistance to ensure compliance with state formalities, instruction on corporate mechanics, and advice on corporate taxation.

Differences between a Corporation and a Partnership

In describing the corporate form, it is useful to compare it to a partnership. Perhaps the most important difference is that, like limited partners, the owners of the corporation—commonly known as shareholders or stockholders—are not personally liable for the corporation's debts; they stand to lose only their investment. But unlike a limited partner, a shareholder is allowed full participation in the control of the corporation through the shareholders' voting privileges.

For the small corporation, however, limited liability may be something of an illusion because very often creditors will require that the owners personally cosign for any credit extended. In addition, individuals remain responsible for their own wrongful acts; thus, a shareholder who negligently causes an injury while engaged in corporate business has not only subjected the corporation to liability but also remains personally liable. However, the corporate liability shield does protect a shareholder from liability for breach of contract, if the other contracting party has agreed to look only to the corporation for responsibility.

The corporate shield also offers protection in situations where an agent hired by the corporation has committed a wrongful act while working for the corporation. If, for example, a management consultant negligently injures a pedestrian while driving somewhere on corporate business, the consultant will be liable for the wrongful act and the corporation *may* be liable, but the shareholders who own the corporation will probably not be personally liable.

The second major difference between a corporation and a partnership relates to continuity of existence. The many events which can cause the dissolution of a partnership do not have the same effect on a corporation. In fact, it is common for "perpetual existence" to be established in the articles of incorporation. Unlike partners, shareholders cannot decide to withdraw and demand a return of capital from the corporation; all they can do is sell their stock. Therefore a corporation may have both legal and economic continuity. But this can also be a tremendous disadvantage to shareholders or their heirs if they want to sell stock when there are no buyers for it. However, agreements can be made which guarantee return of capital to the estate of a shareholder who dies or to a shareholder who decides to withdraw.

The third difference relates to transferability of ownership. No one can become a partner without unanimous consent of the other partners unless otherwise agreed. In a corporation, however, shareholders can generally sell all their shares, or any number of them, to whomever they wish. If the owners of a small corporation do not want it to be open to outside ownership, transferability may be restricted.

The fourth difference is in the structure of management and control. Common shareholders are given a vote in proportion to their ownership in the corporation. Other kinds of stock can be created, with or without voting rights. A voting shareholder uses the vote to elect a board of directors and to create rules under which the board will operate.

The basic rules of the corporation are stated in the articles of incorporation, which are filed with the state. These serve as a sort of constitution, and can be amended by shareholder vote. More detailed operational rules—bylaws—should also be prepared. Both shareholders and directors may have the power to create or amend bylaws. This varies from state to state and may be determined by the shareholders themselves. The board of directors then makes operational decisions for the corporation and might delegate day-to-day control to a president.

A shareholder, even one who owns all the stock, may not pre-empt a decision of the board of directors. If the board has *exceeded* the powers granted it by the articles or bylaws, any shareholder may sue for a court order remedying the situation. But if the board is *within* its powers, the shareholders have no recourse except to remove the board or any board member. In a few more progressive states, a small corporation may entirely forego having a board of directors. In such cases, the corporation is authorized to allow the shareholders to vote on business decisions just as in a partnership.

The fifth distinction between a partnership and a corporation is the greater variety of means available to the corporation for raising additional capital. Partnerships are quite restricted in this regard; they can borrow money or, if all the partners agree, they can take on additional partners. A corporation, on the other hand, may issue more stock, and this stock can be of many different varieties: recallable at a set price, for example, or convertible into another kind of stock.

A means frequently used to attract a new investor is the issuance of preferred stock. The corporation agrees to pay the preferred shareholder some predetermined amount, known as a dividend preference, before it pays any dividends to other shareholders. It also means that if the corporation should go bankrupt, the preferred shareholder will generally be paid out of the proceeds of liquidation before the common shareholders, although after the corporation's creditors are paid.

The issuance of new stock merely requires, in most cases, approval by a majority of the existing shareholders. In addition, corporations can borrow money on a short-term basis by issuing notes, or for a longer period by issuing debentures or bonds. In fact, a corporation's ability to raise additional capital is limited only by its lawyer's creativity and the economics of the marketplace.

The last distinction is the manner in which a corporation is taxed. Under both state and federal laws the profits of the corporation are taxed to the corporation before they are paid out as dividends.

Then, because the dividends constitute income to the shareholders, they are taxed again as personal income. This double taxation constitutes the major disadvantage of incorporating.

Avoiding Double Taxation of Corporate Income

There are several methods of avoiding double taxation. First, a corporation can plan its business so as not to show very much profit. This can be done by drawing off what would be profit in payments to shareholders for a variety of services. For example, a shareholder can be paid a salary, rent for property leased to the corporation, or interest on a loan made to the corporation. All of these are legal deductions from the corporate income.

The corporation can also get larger deductions for the various health and retirement benefits provided for its employees than can an individual or a partnership. For example, a corporation can deduct all of its payments made for an employee health plan while at the same time the employee does not pay any personal income tax on this. Sole proprietors or partnerships can only deduct a much smaller portion of these expenses.

The corporation can also reinvest its profits for reasonable business expansion. This undistributed money is not taxed as income to the individual as it would be if earned by a partnership, which does not distribute it.

Reinvestment has two advantages. First, the business can be built up with money which has been taxed only at the corporate level and on which no individual shareholder needs to pay any tax. Second, the owner can delay the liquidation and distribution of corporate assets until a time of lower personal income and therefore lower tax rates.

The S Corporation

Congress has created a hybrid organizational form which allows the owners of a small corporation to take advantage of many of the features described above but to be taxed like a partnership and avoid the double-taxation problem. This form of organization is called an *S corporation*. If the corporation meets certain requirements, which many small businesses do, the owners can elect to be taxed as if they were a partnership. This can be particularly advantageous in the early years of a corporation because the owners of an S corporation can deduct the losses of the corporation from their personal income, whereas they cannot do that in a standard corporation. They can have this favorable tax situation while simultaneously enjoying the corporation's limited-liability status.

Precautions for Minority Shareholders

Dissolving a corporation is not only painful because of certain tax penalties, it is almost always impossible without the consent of the majority of the shareholders. If you are involved in the formation of a corporation and will be a minority holder you must realize that the majority will have ultimate and absolute control unless minority shareholders take certain precautions from the start. I could relate numerous horror stories of what some majority shareholders have done to minority shareholders. Avoiding these problems is no more difficult than drafting a sort of partnership agreement among the shareholders. I recommend that you retain your own attorney to represent you during the corporation's formation rather than waiting until it is too late.

It is important to determine which business form will be most advantageous for you. This can best be done by consulting with an experienced business lawyer and having your situation evaluated.

In the next chapter I have prepared some questions which you may wish to answer before meeting with your attorney. This should help minimize the amount of attorney's time necessary to create your new business entity.

2

Incorporation Checklist

As discussed in the previous chapter, there are usually two reasons for incorporation: limiting personal liability and minimizing federal income-tax liability. The second reason is generally applicable to a business which is earning a good deal of money. Even if you are not in that category, you may nevertheless want to consider incorporating in order to limit your personal liability.

Corporations are hypothetical legal people and, as such, are responsible for their own acts and contracts. Thus, if the corporation's plant emits noxious fumes, if the corporation's car negligently injures a pedestrian, or if the corporation's product is responsible for lead poisoning, the corporation, not its owners, will be liable if the proper formalities have been adhered to. It should be noted that any individual personally responsible for a wrongful act will also be liable.

Incorporating is generally a fairly simple matter, but to do it right and utilize all the advantages, it is highly recommended that you consult a lawyer. A lawyer's time, of course, is money, but you can save some of that money if you come properly prepared. Here is a checklist of some of the points you will need to discuss with your lawyer.

Certified Public Accountant (CPA)

Other than yourself, the most important person with whom your attorney will work is your accountant. The accountant will provide valuable input on the corporation's financial structure, funding, capitalization, allocation of stock, etc. Your lawyer will be looking to your accountant to provide an opening balance sheet for the corporation from the time that the business moves from sole proprietorship or partnership to corporate status.

Corporate Name

Contact your attorney ahead of time with the proposed name of the corporation. A quick phone call or inquiry to the corporation commissioner or secretary of state in your state capital will reveal whether the proposed corporate name is available. Your attorney can reserve your chosen corporate name until you are ready to use it. You will also have to consider whether the corporation will have a special mark or logo that needs federal trademark protection or state registration. For a discussion of trademarks, see Chapter 12.

Corporate Structure

Who will be the officers of the corporation, i.e., president, vice president, secretary, and treasurer? It may be that the bylaws of the corporation should have a special description for specialized corporate officers. In very small corporations, there probably will not be this elaborate division of responsibilities and titles, but every corporation does need some officers.

State statutes generally require a corporation to have some chief operating officer such as a president. In addition, state corporation laws may require administrative officers such as a secretary, and some state statutes require both.

Shareholders

How many shares should your corporation be authorized to issue? How many shares should be issued at the start of the corporation's business and how many held in reserve for future issuance? Should there be separate classes of shareholders? For example, there may be an occasion when you need to borrow money and want to issue preferred stock to the lender, rather than show the loan as a debt on the books.

If the corporation is to be family owned, stock ownership may be used to some extent as a means of estate planning. You might therefore also wish to ask your attorney about updating your will at the same time you incorporate.

Shareholder Agreements

If your corporation has several shareholde s, is there a method for preventing a shareholders' voting deadlock? You may also wish to discuss with your lawyer possible pre-incorporation shareholder agreements which govern employment status of key shareholders or commit shareholders to voting a certain way on specific corporate issues.

The Buy-Sell Agreement

The first meeting with your lawyer is a good time to discuss buy-sell agreements. What happens when one of the shareholders wishes to leave the business? Under what circumstances should he or she be able to sell to outsiders? In closely held corporations, the corporation or other shareholders are generally granted the first option to buy the stock. What circumstances should trigger the corporation's or other shareholders' right to buy the stock—death, disability, retirement, termination, etc.? Should the buy-sell agreement be tied to key-person insurance that would fund the purchase of stock by the corporation in the event of the death of a key share-holder? What will be the mechanism for valuing stock: annual appraisal, book value, multiple earnings, arbitration, or some other method?

Planning for Future Shareholders

Are there plans to take on new investors or shareholders in the future? Do you have plans for converting the corporation into one which is publicly held, i.e., owned by a large number of investors? If so, the initial structure of the articles of incorporation and stock may be used as an important planning tool for the future.

Capitalization

At this point, the attorney works closely with your CPA. What will the initial capitalization or funding of the corporation be? Will shareholders make loans to the corporation and contribute the rest in exchange for stock? What is being contributed by shareholders in exchange for stock: money, past services, equipment, assets of an ongoing business, licensing agreements, or other things? What value will be placed on assets which are contributed to the corporation?

The Board of Directors

Who will be on the board of directors? How many initial directors will there be? It is a good idea for there to be an odd number in order to avoid the potential for a voting deadlock. Will shareholders have the right to elect members of the board of directors based on their respective stock ownership?

Corporate Housekeeping

Your attorney will need to know several other details. For instance, the number of employees the corporation anticipates for the coming twelve-month period must be stated on the application for a federal tax ID number. Will the corporation's tax year end on December 31 or on another date? Will the corporation's accounting be on a cash basis or accrual basis? Will the corporation authorize salaries for its officers? What will be the date for the annual meeting of the board of directors and shareholders? Who will be the registered agent? Generally your attorney will assume this role.

Employee Benefits

Be prepared to consider employee benefit plans such as life and health insurance, profit sharing, pension or other retirement plans, stock option programs, as well as other fringe benefits. If not implemented when the corporation is created, it is, nonetheless, a good idea to determine when such programs may be instituted.

Chapter S or Section C?

Will the corporation elect to be an S corporation, where income and losses flow directly to shareholders and the corporation pays no income tax, or will it be a standard so-called C corporation where it does pay income tax and corporate income is not taxed to the shareholders? If the corporation is likely to sustain major losses and shareholders have other sources of income against which they wish to write off those losses, chances are the S election would be appropriate.

As you can see, there is much to discuss at the first meeting with your lawyer. A little time and thought prior to that meeting will prove to be a worthwhile investment.

3

The Business Plan

Every business needs capital at one time or another. This funding might be sought as bank loans or other conventional forms of financing, or as venture-capital money, or might be obtained through a public sale of securities, which is discussed more fully in Chapter 5. No matter what the source of financing, an important first step is to prepare a business plan. This can aid a banker or venture capitalist in evaluating your company and can be particularly valuable to the securities lawyer who is representing your company in connection with the securities compliance which may be necessary before you can legally sell any investments in your company.

How to Structure Your Business Plan

The structure and content of the business plan will vary depending upon such factors as the company's stage of development, the nature of the business, and the type of markets it will serve. However, the following topics should be addressed in any business plan.

Executive Summary

This section of the plan should provide the reader with a short overview of the key elements of the business plan. Since sophisticated business people are turned away by exaggeration, the summary must provide an accurate appraisal of the company while distinguishing your product or service and organization from others that are competing for the same funding. It should also describe your management team—emphasizing experience and skills, but not ignoring management weaknesses or how you expect to correct them. Another important part of the summary will be your key financial projections and the funding requirements you will need to meet those projections. Above all, the summary must be designed to catch the reader's attention. Unless the summary inspires one to read on, it has not served its purpose.

Company History

Business people want to know about a company's past performance before they assess its future potential. Toward this end, the business plan should provide a brief history of the company, including: (1) when it was founded, (2) subsequent development and growth, (3) how it has been organized (as a partnership, corporation, or whatever), and (4) how well past performance reflects future potential. If you have good reason to believe that the company's past performance is not indicative of future potential, be sure to state those reasons in this section.

The Product

This section describes in detail the company's products or services, including a summary explanation of any special equipment involved, and a statement about performance and present status. Products which are protected or protectable under the patent, copyright, trademark, or trade-secret laws should also be mentioned in this section. Keep in mind, however, that investors are not likely to have been trained in your field. This section should be written in language easily understandable by business people with nontechnical backgrounds.

The Market

This section should contain a comprehensive description of the market your company plans to serve. If your product is new, independent market research may be needed to define both the initial and future markets. If your product is a refinement of presently available items, the market may already be defined. In that case, you may rely on available data from industry, trade associations, or government sources.

For purposes of obtaining investment capital, the market section may be the most important part of your business plan. To the banker or venture capitalist, a company without a strong understanding of the targeted market is a bad risk, even if its product is first-rate. Consequently, the market description should be longer and more detailed than the product description, indicating to potential investors that you understand the priority of market over product.

The Competition

Identify your competitors, discuss their relative strengths and weaknesses, and indicate the market share held by each. Include a forecast of the market share you expect to capture in the first three to five years, and the competitors from which you expect to draw customers. Be sure to spell out your rationale for each projection— improved product performance, reliability, styling, price, service, or other factors. As with all projections in the business plan, do not understate the strengths of your competition while overestimating your own. Sophisticated business people will not back a company that does not have a realistic view of its competition.

Manufacturing

Efficient production is the key to profit-making. If you manufacture a product, this section should describe your manufacturing facilities and discuss production capacity in relation to projected sales over the first five years. Emphasis should not only be placed on cost reduction, but also on quality control. Minimizing production costs will not make your company more attractive if the savings are offset by increased warranty costs.

Management

As a general rule, bankers and venture capitalists would favor investing in a company with a mediocre product produced by first-rate management over a top-notch product produced by mediocre management. This priority should be reflected in your business plan.

In this section, emphasize the experience of each key management executive. Include job descriptions and salaries, and provide resumes detailing your executives' past business experience, education, publications, and any other information that indicates to potential financers that you have a qualified management team. If your current management team has weak spots, define them and explain how they will be corrected.

Financial Data

First-class products and top-flight management count for nothing if your financial projections do not allow for a substantial return on investment. Consequently, this section is the bottom line of your business plan. Begin by summarizing previous financial performance. If your company is new, be sure that all financial projections are realistic and justifiable. Remember that venture capitalists are sophisticated and will check out other companies in the same field. If your projections deviate widely from the industry norm, you will lose both the credibility and the financing you seek. Furthermore, do not inundate your reader with yards of computer-generated spread sheets. Your financial data should be concise and easy to understand.

Finally, your financial section should discuss the financing itself. Indicate how much money the company needs, the form of the financing sought, and how the money is to be used. Most important, discuss the projected return within the next five years of operation. As with all financial information, be realistic and support your projections with solid data and a sound rationale.

The Business-Plan Team

The development of a well-written business plan is a considerable undertaking. It forces you to focus your ideas, ferret out weak spots in your organization, and turn abstract concepts into concrete plans. Experienced professionals such as lawyers and accountants can provide invaluable assistance in putting together a sound and attractive business plan. Your lawyer can help your company obtain the proper patent, trademark, or trade-secret protection that it needs while steering you away from the legal pitfalls that face all new or expanding businesses. Your CPA can assist you with the myriad financial assessments you must make. A well-known and respected lawyer and accountant can lend credibility to your numbers and projections. Beyond this, experienced lawyers and accountants have invaluable contacts within the venture-capital and banking communities. They can tell you who has the capital, where it is being invested, and how you can best get a share. By enlisting the help of experienced professionals and following the prescribed format, you can develop a business plan that will help you to attract the financing you need for your new or expanding business.

Chapter 4

Borrowing from Banks

Commercial loans can be a valuable source of needed capital for qualified business borrowers.

Lending policies vary dramatically from institution to institution. You should, therefore, talk to several banks to determine which might be likely to lend to your business and which have the most favorable loan terms. While lenders by nature are conservative in their lending policies, you may discover some to be more flexible than others. It makes sense to approach first those banks which are most likely to view your proposal favorably and whose lending criteria you feel you can meet. This will save you time and increase the likelihood that the loan will be approved.

You should not limit your search for a loan to your community. A statewide, regional, or even national search may be necessary before you find the right combination of willing lender and favorable terms.

Having shopped the marketplace and decided on a particular bank, you will be ready for the next step—preparing the loan proposal. The importance of being properly prepared before taking this critical step cannot be overemphasized. Loan officers are not likely to be impressed by a hastily prepared application containing vague, incomplete information and unsubstantiated claims. Many loan requests are doomed at this early stage because ill-prepared applicants failed to adequately present themselves and their businesses to the lender, even though the proposed ventures are in fact sound. What, then, should a borrower understand about the lending process?

The Loan Proposal

Inexperience with the bank's lending procedures can result in an unexpected rejection. Knowing the bank's lending policy and following its procedure is, therefore, essential. Just what does a lender look for in a loan application? At a minimum, a borrower should be prepared to satisfactorily address each of the following questions:

1. Is your business "credit-worthy"?
2. Do you need a short-term or long-term loan? For what purpose?
3. How much money do you really need?
4. What kind of collateral do you and your business have to secure the loan?
5. What are the lender's rules and what limitations would attach to this loan?

The lender's decision to grant or refuse the loan request will be based on your answers to these questions.

Is Your Business Credit-Worthy?

The ability to obtain money when you need it may be as important to the operation of your business as having a good location and the right equipment. But before an institution will agree to lend you money, the loan officer must be satisfied that you and your business constitute a good risk—that is, that you are credit-worthy. This decision will include several considerations.

Good Character. The lender will want to know what sort of person you are. Do you have a good reputation in the community and in your business? Are you known in the community? What is your past credit history and what is the likelihood that you will repay the loan if your business falters or even fails?

Despite its subjective nature, this character factor figures prominently in the lender's decision-making. It is not uncommon for a loan officer to deny a loan request, regardless of how qualified the applicant appears on paper, if the officer is not convinced of the borrower's good character. Even for "signature loans"—which require only the applicant's signature and are available only to businesses and entrepreneurs with the highest credit standing, business integrity, and management skills—the applicant's character will affect the institution's decision to make a loan, even when well collateralized.

What Is the Money Needed for? Is the money needed to purchase inventory? Or to acquire fixed assets, such as machinery or equipment? The answer to this will determine what type of loan—long-term or short-term—the applicant should request. Loans needed to purchase inventory, especially where the applicant's business is highly seasonal, will generally be short-term loans, requiring repayment within one year or less. This is because the bank will likely anticipate repayment from the sale of the assets financed by the loan.

Intermediate-term loans, requiring payment between one and five years, and long-term loans, those extending payments over ten or even fifteen years, are more appropriate for purchases of fixed assets, since repayment is expected to be made not from the sale of these assets but from the earnings generated by the company's ongoing use of them. Those assets produce income at a much slower rate, hence the bank's willingness to allow repayment over a longer period. Bear in mind that commercial lenders are interested in offering funds to successful businesses in need of additional capital to expand and increase profitability. They are not particularly inclined to make loans to businesses needing the money to pay off existing debts.

When and How Will the Loan Be Repaid? When and how the loan will be repaid is closely associated with the preceding questions of how much money is needed and for what purpose. The banker will now use judgment and professional experience to assess your business ability and the likelihood of your future success. The banker will want to know whether or not the proposed use of the borrowed funds justifies the repayment schedule requested. You as the borrower *must* be able to demonstrate that the cash flow anticipated from the proceeds of the loan will be adequate to meet the repayment terms if the loan is granted.

Is the Cushion on the Loan Large Enough?

The lender will want to know if the borrower has included in the loan request a suitable allowance for unexpected business developments. That is, does the loan proposal realistically allow for the vissicitudes of operating a business and provide for alternative resources to meet the borrower's obligation if the business expectations are not met? Or is the borrower stretching to the limit, leaving no margin for error, so that repayment can be made only if the proposed venture is successful? In the latter circumstance, the lender may consider the loan too risky.

The Business Outlook

The lender will be evaluating the business outlook for your company in particular, and for your type of business in general, in light of contemporary economic realities. Can your proposed use of the loan be reasonably expected to produce the anticipated increased revenues for your business? While your proposed plan may appear viable on paper, it may not be realistic given the state of the economy within which your company operates.

Financial Evidence

Remember that bankers prefer to make loans to solvent, profitable, growing enterprises. They seek assurance that the loan will contribute to that growth since your repayment ability is directly related to your success. As noted previously, bankers are not interested in lending money so that a business can pay off already existing loans. To aid the bank in understanding the financial health of your business, you probably will be asked to provide specific financial data. Two basic financial documents are customarily submitted for this purpose: the balance sheet and the profit and loss statement. The balance sheet will aid the bank in evaluating your business's solvency, while the profit and loss statement summarizes the business's current performance. Unless yours is a new venture, you should be prepared to submit these financial reports for at least the past two or three years, since they are the principal means for measuring your company's stability and growth potential. Ideally, these statements will have been prepared by an independent Certified Public Accountant (CPA).

Analyzing Your Business Potential

In interviewing loan applicants and in studying the financial records of their businesses, the bank is especially interested in the following facts and figures.

General Information

Are the company books and financial records up to date, accurate and in good condition, or are they incomplete, infrequently maintained and in disarray? Haphazard recordkeeping not only fails to reflect the business's true financial state, but demonstrates poor managerial skills. For obvious reasons, banks are reluctant to back poorly run businesses, viewing them as too risky.

The lender will also be interested in the current condition of your business accounts payable and notes payable. Are those obligations being paid in a timely fashion or are they overdue? If you are not presently able to meet existing debts, the lender will be hard pressed to understand how you expect to be able to meet any additional obligations. Perhaps the requested funds will solve cash-flow problems you now have and will also increase earnings so that you will be able to bring past-due accounts current while adequately handling the added debt. In this situation, you might overcome the lender's skepticism by presenting a well-thought-out, solid business plan that clearly demonstrates how the new loan will solve, rather than add to, the business's financial problems and will boost revenues.

Additionally, the lender will likely want to know the salaries of the owner/manager and other company officers to see if they are reasonable. Excessive salaries represent an unacceptable drain on company resources and profits, which may adversely affect the company's ability to meet debt obligations.

The lender will also be interested in the size of your work force. Does it seem adequate to maximize the business's potential or does it seem excessive compared to other, similar businesses?

You should be prepared to discuss the adequacy of your company's insurance coverage, your present tax situation (whether all taxes are current) and, if your business sells a product, what the size is, if any, of your order backlog.

All of these factors say something about the financial state of your business. Although the lender may inquire into other areas, the borrower who knows the type of general information of interest to a lender and can present it articulately greatly increases the chances of having the loan approved.

Accounts Receivable

Of particular interest to the bank will be the number of customers that are behind in their payments to you and how far behind they are. The lender will also want to know what percent of your company's total accounts receivable are owed by customers that are currently behind in their payments, as well as whether a major account is behind, in which event the bank will want to know the likelihood that this account will eventually be paid. The accounts receivable situation is of special interest to a lender when the borrower is relying on those accounts to provide the cash flow needed to service the requested loan.

You should also expect the potential lender to ask if your business has an adequate cash reserve to cover questionable accounts and whether the accounts receivable have already been pledged as collateral. A lender who secures a loan with collateral that has already been pledged to a prior lender will, in most cases, be limited in its ability to foreclose on that collateral if the debtor defaults. The prior lender has first right to liquidate the collateral, while subsequent lenders will receive only those proceeds remaining after the prior debt is fully satisfied.

Inventory

If the applicant's business involves the sale of goods, the bank will need to know the current state of the inventory on hand. Is it in good shape or will it have to be marked down before sale? Is the inventory raw materials or the finished product? Banks are interested in unpledged inventory as a possible source of collateral and also as a source of future revenues. The bank may also be interested in the inventory turnover rate, which reflects the demand for your product and aids in evaluating the accuracy of your revenue projections.

Fixed Assets

Since fixed assets can be used to secure the loan, the bank will likely be interested in the type, condition, age, and current market value of your company's equipment, machinery, and so on. You should be prepared to explain how these assets have been depreciated, their useful life expectancy, and whether they have been previously mortgaged or pledged as collateral to another lender. In addition, be ready to discuss any need or plans to acquire fixed assets. On the one hand, this need could mean additional debt obligations in the near future; on the other, it could explain and justify your projected growth.

Options for Owners of New Businesses

This analysis applies primarily to loan requests made by established, proven businesses. New-business loan applicants probably will not be able to supply much of the information described here, which will not necessarily preclude having a loan approved, but could make its approval more difficult. You should, however, be aware that new-business loans constitute only approximately 5 percent of all business loans made.

This reluctance to finance unproven businesses, understandably frustrating to new-business owners, is consistent with the traditionally conservative nature of banks, which owe a fiduciary duty to their stockholders and depositers to disburse funds in a prudent, responsible manner. In light of the extraordinarily high failure rate of new businesses, compounded by the fact that a new business generally cannot provide adequate financial data to evaluate its potential for success, the lender is hard pressed to justify making many high-risk-type loans. Even where the new-business borrower offers more than adequate collateral to secure the loan, the request may be denied.

Banks are comfortable lending money and earning profits from the interest charged on their loans. They are not comfortable in the role of an involuntary partner in the failing business of a delinquent debtor. Even though banks secure loans with a wide range of collateral, they understandably are not anxious to have to foreclose on that security. They are not in the business of selling business machinery or inventory, or of trying to collect a delinquent debtor's accounts receivable. Although banks try to protect themselves by lending only a fraction of the collateral's market value, they still may not obtain the full amount that they are owed in a "distress sale" of that collateral, since this type of sale traditionally attracts bargain-hunters who will often buy only at prices well below true market value. With an understanding of these dynamics, a new-business loan applicant can better appreciate a bank's hestitation in approving a loan.

However, banks do make some loans to new businesses. The entrepreneur will need to demonstrate a good reputation for paying debts and offer evidence of business-management skills. Perhaps you have first-hand knowledge and expertise in the type of business you propose to establish as a result of having been previously employed in the same or a closely related field. Emphasize that. In addition, provide a sound business plan to support your projections. You can further improve your chances of obtaining a loan if you have invested your own money in the business, thus indicating your confidence in its success. Furthermore, show, if possible, that the business has a good debt-equity ratio and that it is not saddled with an inordinately high debt.

Even if your loan is initially refused, it is important to establish a good working relationship with a bank. Any initial business success will impress upon the bank the soundness of your plan, thereby opening the door for future financing should the need arise.

Short-Term or Long-Term Financing?

Once the bank has evaluated the credit-worthiness of your business, you should be ready to explain the appropriateness of the kind of loan requested. I mentioned this topic briefly above, but it deserves some additional attention. It is important to be able to convince the lender that your proposed use of the borrowed money will generate the additional revenue needed to repay the loan during the repayment period. Short-term loans are appropriate for purchasing inventory or facilitating collection of outstanding accounts receivable. They are expected to be repaid when the inventory is sold or the accounts are collected. Long-term loans are customarily used to finance acquisition of fixed assets. This would justify a longer repayment period since the newly acquired assets will generate additional earnings more slowly. Depending upon your credit reputation, short-term loans may be available with or without security. It is more likely that long-term loans will require adequate security, often necessitating a pledge of some or all of your assets.

How Much Money Will You Need?

The lender is also concerned with the amount of the loan since an undercapitalized business is likely to get into financial trouble. Similarly, a lender will be reluctant to approve a loan which is excessive, since the debt service may result in an unnecessarily high cash drain on the company. The loan should net the borrower the amount necessary to accomplish the desired goal with a slight cushion for error and no more. Estimating the amounts needed to finance building construction, conversion, or expansion—long-term loans—is relatively easy, as is estimating the cost of fixed-asset acquisition. On the other hand, working-capital needs—short-term loans—are more difficult to assess and depend upon your type of business. To plan your working-capital requirements, it is important to know the cash flow of your business, present and anticipated. This involves simply a projection of all the elements of cash receipts and disbursements at the time they are likely to occur. These figures should be projected monthly to aid the bank in its evaluation.

What Kind of Collateral Do Lenders Require?

Sometimes loans will be made solely on the borrower's signature. More frequently, banks will require collateral to secure the loan. Acceptable collateral can take a variety of forms. The type and amount of collateral necessary in a given situation will depend on the particular bank's lending policies and the borrower's financial state. In general, banks will accept the following types of collateral as security for a business loan.

Endorsers', Co-makers' or Guarantors' Promises to Pay. You may have to get other people to sign a note in order to bolster your credit. These people—sureties—may co-sign your note as endorsers, co-makers or guarantors. While the law makes some subtle distinctions as to when each of these sureties becomes liable for the borrower's debt, in essence those parties will be expected to pay back the borrowed funds if you are unable to do so. The bank may or may not require sureties to pledge their own assets as security for the promise to pay upon your default. This will depend, to a great extent, on the surety's own financial situation.

Assignment of Leases. Assigning a lease as a form of security is particularly appropriate for franchise situations. If the bank lends a franchise money for a building and takes back a mortgage, that mortgage may be secured by assigning to the lender the lease entered into between the franchisor and the franchisee that will occupy the building. If the franchisor fails to meet mortgage payments, the bank can directly receive the franchisee's lease payments in satisfaction of the franchisor's debt.

Warehouse Receipts. Banks will accept commodities as security by lending money on a warehouse receipt. Such a receipt is usually delivered directly to the bank and shows that the merchandise used as security either has been placed in a public warehouse or has been left on your premises under control of a bonded employee. Such loans are generally made only on standard, readily marketable goods.

Chattel Mortgages. Equipment loans may be secured by giving the bank a lien on the equipment you are buying. The amount loaned will likely be less than the purchase price. How much less will be determined by the present and future market value of the equipment and its rate of depreciation. You will be expected to adequately insure the equipment and to properly maintain it and protect it from damage.

Real Estate Holdings. You may be able to borrow against the equity in your personal real estate holdings as well as those of the business, though you will likely be required to maintain the property in good condition and carry adequate insurance on the property for the benefit of the lender at least up to the amount of the loan.

Accounts Receivable. Many banks will lend money secured by your business's accounts receivable. In effect, the bank is relying on your customers to pay off your note obligation to the bank.

Savings Accounts and Life Insurance Policies. Sometimes you may get a loan by assigning your savings account to the lender. Here, the lender will keep your passbook while notifying the savings account holder of the existence of the debt in order to ensure that the account will not be diminished during the term of the loan. Loans can also be made up to the cash value of a life insurance policy, but you must be prepared to assign the policy over to the lender.

Stocks and Bonds. Stocks and bonds may be accepted as collateral for a loan if they are readily marketable. However, banks will likely lend no more than 75 percent of the market value of a high-grade security. If the value of the securities drops below the lender's required margin, the borrower may be asked to provide additional security for the loan.

Inventory. As discussed above, business inventory, either on hand or to be acquired in the future, can be used as security for short-term loans. The lender will expect the loan to be repaid from the revenues generated by the sale of this inventory on a timely basis. Inventory may also be used as collateral for long-term loans when the lender establishes a so-called *field warehousing* arrangement. In this situation the inventory is segregated and identified as collateral for a loan with an employee, responsible to the lender, placed in charge of the field warehouse.

Lender's Rules and Limitations

Once the loan has been approved in principal, it is likely that the bank will impose certain rules and constraints on you and your business. These serve to protect the lender against unnecessary risk and against the possibility of your engaging in poor management practices. You, your attorney, and your business advisor should evaluate all of the terms and conditions of the loan in order to determine whether it is acceptable. If the bank's requirements are too onerous, it may be appropriate for you to decline this loan and seek alternative financing. Never agree to restrictions to which you cannot realistically adhere. If, on the other hand, the terms and conditions of the loan are acceptable, even though they are demanding, it would be appropriate to take the loan. In fact, some borrowers view these limitations as an opportunity for improving their own management techniques and business profitability.

Especially in making long-term loans, the lender will be interested in the net earning power of the borrowing company, the capability of its management, the long-range prospects of the company, and the long-range prospects of the industry of which the company is a part.

As a result of the bank's scrutiny of your company, the kinds of limitations imposed will depend, to a great extent, on the company itself. If the company is a good risk, only minimum limitations need be set. A poor risk, of course, should expect greater limitations to be placed on it.

There are three common types of limitations you are likely to encounter.

Repayment Terms. The bank will want to set a loan-repayment

schedule that accurately reflects your ability to earn revenues sufficient to meet the proposed obligation. Risky businesses can expect
shorter terms, while proven enterprises may receive longer periods
within which to repay the loan.

Use of Pledged Security. Once a lender agrees to accept collateral
to secure a loan, it will understandably be keenly interested in assur-
ing that, should the need arise, the collateral will still be available to
satisfy the debt. To this end, the lender may take actual possession
of the collateral if it is stocks, bonds, or other negotiable instru-
ments. Of course, a bank is not likely to take physical possession of
a business's inventory or fixed assets, and remove them to the
bank's vault.

There are, however, other ways by which a bank can obtain possession of your fixed assets while allowing you to use them. For example, the lender could "perfect"—legally establish—a *security interest* in machinery and equipment used in your plant by filing a
financing statement in the appropriate state or county office. (A
security interest is the legal term for a lender's rights in collateral.)
Real estate mortgages are perfected by having them recorded in the
appropriate government offices, and security interests in inventory
can be perfected for most purposes by either filing a financing statement or establishing a field warehousing system, or both. In these
situations, the bank may impose restrictions on the use of the collateral and require that it be properly maintained and adequately insured. The bank may further limit or prohibit you from pledging the
same collateral for any other business debts or loans.

While this sounds reasonable, you should recognize that such restrictions may seriously hamper your ability to borrow additional
funds should the need arise at a future time. For example, where inventory is used as collateral, you must find out exactly how much of
your inventory is involved. A bank may ask for only a percentage of
the total inventory to secure the loan. More likely, though, the
bank's security interest will extend to all of the company's inventory
on hand at any given time, including any later-acquired supplies.

Here lies the potential problem. The inventory's value may well exceed the amount of the loan which it secures. Nonetheless, you may find yourself in the position of not being able to use any of the inventory as collateral for any additional loans. In cases where this situation is likely to arise, you are well advised to consider alternative sources of collateral.

Periodic Reporting. To protect itself, a lender may require you to supply it with certain financial statements on a regular basis, perhaps quarterly or even monthly. From these, the lender can see if, in fact, the business is performing up to the expectations projected in the loan application. This type of oversight serves not only to reassure the lender that the loan will be repaid, but also to identify and help solve problems early on before they become insurmountable and threaten the business's viability.

Details of the Agreement

The loan agreement itself is a tailor-made document—a contract between the lender and borrower—that spells out in detail all the terms and conditions of the loan. The actual restrictions placed on the loan will be found in the agreement under a section entitled "Covenants." Negative covenants are things that you may not do without the lender's prior approval, such as incurring additional debt or pledging the loan's collateral or other business assets to another lender as collateral for a second loan. On the other hand, positive covenants spell out those things which you must do, such as carry adequate insurance, provide specified financial reports and repay the loan according to the terms of the loan agreement. Note that, with the lender's prior consent, the terms and conditions contained in the loan agreement can be amended, adjusted, or even waived. Remember that you can negotiate the loan terms with the lender before signing. True, the bank is in the superior position but legitimate lenders are happy to cooperate with qualified borrowers.

The Loan Application

Having targeted your source for funds and analyzed the business in terms you now know lenders look at, you are ready to develop the loan request. Though most lenders will require the application to include the same standard, essential information, they often differ as to the proper format of the application. Some lenders may provide suggested formats; others may require a specific format. The actual content, length and formality will depend on the lender's familiarity with your business, the amount of money requested, and the proposed use of the borrowed funds. A simple application form and a conversation may be adequate for your local banker. The start-up business seeking substantial funds from lenders unfamiliar with it will be required to provide much more extensive documentation, including a detailed plan of the entire business.

The business loan applicant can expect to be asked to submit any or all of the following information:

1. Personal financial statements. These will indicate the applicant's personal net worth. This is helpful in evaluating creditworthiness and revealing potential sources of collateral, as well as estimating repayment capabilities.
2. Recent and current tax filings of the individual and of the business.
3. The business's financial statements. These, as mentioned above, ideally should extend back for at least two or three years and should have been prepared and authenticated by an independent CPA. Cash flow statements and profit projections may also be requested by the lender.
4. A business history. This should include past profit or loss patterns, current debt-to-equity ratio, current and projected cash flow and present and projected future earnings.
5. A business plan. This should explain the proposed use of the requested funds and explain how the loan will benefit the business. The length and content of this plan will vary according to the financial health of the applicant's business and the amount and type of loan applied for.

Other documentation may also be requested. The individual lender will be able to indicate what is needed in light of the given circumstances.

Importance of Communication When Problems Arise

Once a loan is approved and disbursed, the borrower must address a new set of obligations and liabilities. Of course, if all goes according to plan, the business will prosper, the loan will be repaid on schedule, and all concerned parties will be happy. However, the business world is fraught with uncertainty. If the business falters and revenues tumble, the borrower may not be able to meet the debt obligations. If this occurs, it becomes imperative that the borrower react responsibly, viewing the lender as a potential ally in solving problems rather than as an adversary. At least initially, bankers are not eager to exercise their right to foreclose on the collateral securing the loan at the first indication that the debt may not be repaid. They likely have no experience in marketing the types of collateral involved, nor do they want to run a distress sale, which at best would probably bring in only a fraction of the money owed. Additionally, foreclosing against the business's assets further decreases the bank's chance of recovering any of the unpaid balance since now the borrower, having been stripped of the means to carry on the business, is likely to be bankrupt. Even if the lender can liquidate the collateral at its current fair market value, that value may be well below the value agreed upon when the loan was made. For these and other reasons, banks foreclose on collateral only as a last resort.

Bear in mind that, in general, lenders prefer to work with a potentially defaulting debtor to help ease the debt burden so that the borrower can overcome the problems, stay in business, and reestablish the enterprise's profitability. To this end, lenders, through experience, have learned to identify a variety of red flags as indications that the debtor is experiencing financial difficulty. For example, the alert is sounded when loan payments start to be made later and later each month, or when the business's account increasingly shows checks being dishonored for insufficient funds.

When the lender sees these signals, the account may be assigned to a separate department set up within the bank to assist borrowers in overcoming problems. The bank may be willing to offer a variety of accommodations to help the borrower; repayment terms can be extended, the amount of payment due each month can be temporarily reduced, or the bank may accept repayment of interest only, until the business has overcome its temporary difficulties. The bank may be in a position to offer advice for ways to help solve the business's problems, particularly where poor management is the source of the difficulties.

How far and to what extent the bank will be willing to accommodate a delinquent debtor very often depends on the attitude and degree of cooperation of the debtor. Hard-pressed debtors often fail to understand the importance of establishing a cooperative, rather than an adversarial, relationship with the lender. At the first sign of trouble, the borrower should take the initiative to notify the bank and explain what is being done to remedy the situation. Expecting a bank to be sympathetic to one's plight and make concessions seems unreasonable in cases where the borrower waits until the debt is long past due before approaching the lender to explain the problems. Additionally, a bank is not likely to be too sympathetic toward a borrower who fails to return phone calls and virtually disappears, always "unavailable" to discuss the problem with the bank.

The lender is likely to be most cooperative with a hard-pressed debtor who early on alerts the bank to the problems, explains what efforts are being made to remedy them, and keeps in close contact with the bank, informing it of current developments and of the progress made toward solution of the problems.

A favorably impressed lender can be an invaluable asset to your business, not only in granting loans but in helping you out in difficult times. Do not underestimate the need for establishing a solid professional relationship with your lender. The ultimate success and growth of your business may well depend on it.

5

Going Public

Each year, hundreds of private businesses go public. In the first eight months of 1984 (the latest priod for which figures are available), 262 companies raised approximately $2.52 billion through their initial public offerings. However, some small companies have become disillusioned with the supposed benefits of going public and are returning to their former private status. It is worthwhile to look at the pros and cons of going public and some of the factors you should consider before making that crucial decision.

Advantages of Going Public

Access to capital and increased prestige are the motivating forces behind going public.

Issuing stock has the advantage of raising much-needed capital without draining the resources needed for daily operations. The additional capital allows for continued growth even when earnings and bank loans are insufficient to meet expansion objectives. Also, a successful public offering can improve net worth and debt-to-equity ratio, thereby increasing credibility and financing leverage with lenders.

Public offerings also enhance a company's prestige by increasing its visibility within the business community. The prestige of issuing stock is an effective device for attracting top-rate management executives. In turn, a strong management team is often the key to attracting new investors.

Disadvantages of Going Public

Disadvantages of going public are primarily high costs and diminished control over the company.

The cost of going public includes extensive fees for printing, attorneys, accountants, filing fees, and underwriter commissions. Businesses contemplating a public offering should expect an initial outlay of $50,000 to $150,000. In addition, going public increases a business's administrative costs. Going public means more regulations to adhere to, and more paperwork to process. Public corporations undergo extensive auditing and must gather and disseminate information for their shareholders. These additional administrative functions add to the overall cost of doing business.

While shareholders supply much-needed capital to a growing business, they also usurp a degree of control over the company's operations. Suddenly, management is beholden to a large number of investors whose interest in short-term profits may conflict with what is best for the long-term health of the business. Shareholders must also be apprised of otherwise private information—details about management, organization, executives, products, sales, and profit figures. Public divulgence of this information can put a business at a competitive disadvantage. Furthermore, minority shareholders have certain dissenter and minority rights that give them a voice disproportionate to the size of their holdings. These disadvantages—high costs and diminished control over the business—must be carefully weighed before taking on the rigors of going public.

The Initial Public Offering

Deciding to go public and implementing that decision is a time-consuming and complicated task. A company must first determine whether it is in an appropriate position to make a public offering, and then choose the optimal time. Factors to consider include the availability of other means of financing, the degree of financial need, and market conditions for the specific product or services being offered. Since an initial public offering (IPO) is highly complex, any business proceeding with an IPO needs to assemble a professional team to assist with the myriad legal and financial considerations which invariably arise. This support team should include experienced legal counsel, independent accountants, investment bankers, underwriters, and selling agents.

Federal and State Securities Laws

The complex nature of securities law underscores the need for experienced legal counsel. Those laws are promulgated under both state and federal statutes.

The Securities and Exchange Commission (SEC) is responsible for administering federal securities laws. Its purpose is to assure equal access to and full disclosure of all material facts about a business. However, the SEC recognizes that the burden of disclosure is often excessive and nonessential as applied to smaller businesses. Consequently, special procedures and exemptions have been established for small businesses to simplify and expedite the registration process.

In addition to federal securities regulation each state has its own securities laws, known as "blue sky" laws. Compliance with federal law does not end the matter. You must also comply with state provisions, which are sometimes even more stringent. Consequently, stricter state provisions regarding the registration of small issues may offset the benefits of simplified procedures and exemptions under federal law. Nevertheless, stricter state provisions must be complied with.

Violations of securities laws can result in civil or, in some cases, criminal liability. Sanctions include rescission (refund) of the entire offering, money damages, injunction against or voiding of business transactions, and even criminal prosecution. Furthermore, all securities, whether registered or exempt, are subject to strict anti-fraud provisions. Liability of the issuer is unlimited and extends to significant shareholders and other related persons or entities as well.

The Attorney's Role

The extremely complex nature of securities law makes the experienced attorney an indispensable part of any successful public offering. The attorney must ensure that all relevant laws and regulations are adhered to. Attorneys must also make the company aware of possible exemptions, advise on necessary disclosures, and assist in preparing the necessary disclosure document, for instance a prospectus and a registration statement. Furthermore, an experienced attorney can review existing contracts and advise changes, file necessary documents for SEC review, and recommend internal structural changes that will ease the company's transition from private to public.

6

Contracts

Contracts constitute a fundamental legal and practical problem in virtually every business. Clearly, we cannot cover here the entire field of contract law, but perhaps I can help you become aware of some of the ramifications of contract law and enable you to see where you need protection.

What Is a Contract?

A contract is a legally binding promise or set of promises. The law requires that the parties to a contract perform the promises they have made to each other. In the event of nonperformance—usually called a *breach*—the law provides remedies to the injured party. For the purposes of this discussion, we will assume that the contract is between two people, though it can involve business organizations as well.

The three basic elements of every contract are the *offer*, the *acceptance*, and the *consideration*. For example, suppose a salesperson shows a customer a Mustang convertible at an automobile lot and suggests that she buy it (the offer). The customer says she likes it and wants it (the acceptance). They agree on a price (the consideration).

That is the basic framework, but a great many variations can be played on that theme.

Types of Contracts

Contracts may be *express* or *implied*; they may be *oral* or *written*. On this latter point, there are at least two types of contracts that *must* be in writing if they are to be legally enforceable: (1) any contract which, by its terms, cannot be completed in less than one year, and (2) any contract that involves the sale of goods for over $500.

An express contract is one in which all the details are spelled out. For example, you might make a contract with a retail store for six dozen gallons of apple cider to be delivered by you on October 1, at a price of $1.75 per gallon, to be paid for within 30 days of receipt.

That is fairly straightforward. If either party fails to live up to any material part of the contract, a breach has occurred, and the other party may withhold performance of his or her obligation until receiving assurance that the breaching party will perform. In the event no such assurance is forthcoming, the aggrieved party may have a cause of action and go to court for breach of contract.

If the apple cider is delivered on October 15 and the store had advertised the availability of your special apple cider during the week of October 1, time was an important consideration and the store would not be required to accept the late shipment. But if time is not a material consideration, then even with the slight delay this probably would be considered "substantial performance" and the store would have to accept the delivery.

Express contracts can be either oral or written, though if you are going to the trouble of expressing contractual terms, you should put your understanding in writing.

Implied contracts need not be very complicated, either, though they are usually not done in writing. An example might be if you call a supplier to order five boxes of computer paper without making any express statement that you will pay for the paper. The promise to pay is implied in the order, and is enforceable when the paper is delivered.

But with implied contracts, things can often become a lot stickier. Suppose a manufacturer of notepads asks you to send over a supply of a new kind of glue you have just begun marketing, to try it out. You deliver a generous amount. The notepad manufacturer likes the glue and uses it up, and is overheard commenting that it is the best glue yet for the manufacture of notepads.

Is there an implied contract to purchase in this arrangement? That may depend on whether you are normally in the business of giving away large free samples of new products.

You enter into many contracts without thinking much about them, such as those exchanges of promises which take place between your business and the company supplying your telephone service. (The telephone company agrees to provide certain telecommunications services in exchange for your promise to pay for those services under certain agreed-upon terms.)

Perhaps the more problematic contracts are those which you enter into on a regular but intermittent basis for the purchase or sale of goods and services critical to the ongoing viability and smooth running of your business.

Let us examine the principles of offer, acceptance, and consideration in the context of several potential situations for a hypothetical business owner, Pat Smith.

Smith is an automobile dealer who has an impressive collection of vintage cars restored to mint condition. We will look at the following situations and see whether an enforceable contract comes into existence.

At a cocktail party, Jones expresses an interest in Smith's cars. "It looks like the market value of your cars keeps going up," Jones tells Smith. "I'm going to buy one while I can still afford it."

Is this a contract? If so, what are the terms of the offer—the particular car, the specific price? No, this is not really an offer that Smith can accept. It is nothing more than an opinion or a vague expression of intent.

Brown offers to pay $4,000 for one of Smith's cars that she saw in an auto show several weeks ago. At the show, it was listed at $4,500, but Smith agrees to accept the lower price.

Is this an enforceable contract? Yes! Brown has offered, in unambiguous terms, to pay a specific amount for a specific car, and Smith has accepted the offer. A binding contract exists.

One day Jones shows up at Smith's vintage-auto lot and sees a particular car for which he offers $4,500. Smith accepts and promises to transfer title the next week, at which time Jones will pay for it. An hour later, Brown shows up. She likes the same car and offers Smith $6,000 for it. Can Smith accept the later offer?

No—a contract exists with Jones. An offer was made and accepted. The fact that the object has not yet been delivered or paid for does not make the contract any less binding.

Green discusses certain renovations he would like Smith to perform on a particular car Smith has just acquired. He offers to pay $6,000 for the car if the final product is satisfactory to him. Green approves preliminary sketches, and Smith completes the work. But when Green shows up to pick up his car, he refuses to accept it because it does not satisfy him.

Green is making the offer in this case, but the offer is conditional upon his satisfaction with the completed work. Smith can only accept the offer by producing something that meets Green's subjective standards—a risky business. There is no enforceable contract for payment until such time as Green indicates that the completed work is satisfactory.

Suppose Green comes to Smith's vintage-car lot and says that the car is satisfactory but then, when Smith delivers it, says he has changed his mind. That is too late. The contract became binding at the moment he indicated the work to be satisfactory. If he then refuses to accept it, he would be breaching his contract.

Earlier I mentioned that contracts for goods over $500 must be in writing. The example just above was of a hybrid sale, for goods and services. Since the goods involved were over $500 in value, the contract should be in writing to ensure enforceability. However, if the contract had been one for performance of personal services only

—say, for renovation to be performed by Smith on Green's own car
—the Uniform Commercial Code (UCC) would not apply and the
contract would be enforceable whether it was reduced to writing or
not. (The Uniform Commercial Code is a compilation of commercial laws enacted in every state except Louisiana.)

Oral or Written Contracts?

Contracts are enforceable only if they can be proven. All of the
hypothetical examples mentioned above could have been oral contracts, but a great deal of detail is often lost in the course of remem-
bering a conversation. The best practice, of course, is to get it in
writing. The function of a written contract is not only that of proof,
but to make very clear the understanding of the parties regarding
the agreement and the terms of the contract.

Some smaller-business owners prefer to do business strictly on
the basis of so-called "gentlemen's agreements," particularly with
their immediate suppliers and retailers. The assumption seems to be
that the best business relations are those based upon mutual trust
alone.

Although there may be some validity to this, business owners
nevertheless really should put all oral agreements into writing. Far
too many trusting people have suffered adverse consequences because of their idealistic reliance upon the sanctity of oral contracts.

Under even the best of business relationships, it is still possible
that one or both parties might forget the terms of an oral agreement. Or both parties might have quite different perceptions about
the precise terms of the agreement reached. When, however, the
agreement is put into writing, there is much less doubt as to the
terms of the arrangement, although even a written contract may
contain ambiguities if it is not drafted with considerable care. Thus
a written contract generally functions as a safeguard against subsequent misunderstanding or forgetful minds.

Perhaps the principal problem with oral contracts lies in the fact
that they cannot always be proven or enforced.

Proof of oral contracts typically centers around the conflicting
testimony of the parties involved. And if one of the parties is not

able to establish by a preponderance of evidence that his or her version of the contract is the correct one, then the oral contract may be considered nonexistent—as though it had never been made. The same result might ensue if the parties cannot remember the precise terms of the agreement, and memories do fade.

When Written Contracts Are Necessary

Even if an oral contract is established, it may not always be enforceable. As already noted, there are some agreements which must be in writing in order to be legally enforceable.

An early law that was designed to prevent fraud and perjury, known as the Statute of Frauds, provides that any contract which by its terms cannot be fully performed within one year must be in writing. This rule is narrowly interpreted, so if there is *any* possibility, no matter how remote, that the contract *could* be fully performed within one year, the contract need not be reduced to writing.

For example, if a jeweler agreed to submit one piece of custom-designed jewelry to a customer each year for a period of five years, the contract would have to be in writing since by the very terms of the agreement there is no way the contract could be performed within one year. If, on the other hand, the contract called for the jeweler to deliver five pieces within a period of five years, the contract would not have to be in writing under the Statute of Frauds, since it is possible, though perhaps not probable, that the jeweler would deliver all five pieces within the first year. The fact that the jeweler does not actually complete performance of the contract within one year is immaterial. So long as complete performance within one year is within the realm of possibility, the contract need not be in writing to be enforceable; it may be oral.

The Statute of Frauds further provides that any contract for the sale of goods valued at $500 or more is not enforceable unless it has been put into writing and signed by the party against whom enforcement is being sought. The fact that a contract for a price in excess of $500 is not in writing does not void the agreement or render it illegal. The parties are free to perform the oral arrangement, but, if one party refuses to perform, the other will be unable to legally enforce the agreement.

The law defines *goods* as all things that are movable at the time of making the contract except for the money used as payment. The real question becomes whether a particular contract involves the sale of goods for a price of $500 or more. Although the answer would generally seem to be fairly clear, ambiguities may arise.

For example, if a supplier agrees to provide a business with all its stationery needs for the coming year, how is the price to be determined? Or if the jeweler sells a number of pieces to a customer where the total purchase price exceeds $500 but the price of the individual works is less than $500, which price governs? In light of these possible ambiguities the safest course is to put all oral contracts into writing.

No-Cost Written Agreements

At this point, owners of small businesses might object, asserting that they do not have the time, energy, or patience to draft contracts. After all, they are in business to make a product or sell a service, not to formulate written contracts steeped in legal jargon.

Fortunately, the business person will not always be required to do this, since the supplier or retailer may be willing to draft a satisfactory contract. However, be wary of signing any form contracts— *they will almost invariably be one-sided*, with all terms in favor of whoever paid to have them drafted.

As a second alternative, the business person could employ an attorney to draft contracts. But this might be worthwhile only for substantial transactions. With respect to smaller transactions, the legal fees may be much larger than the benefits derived from having a written contract.

The Uniform Commercial Code provides businesses with a third and perhaps the best alternative. Businesses need not draft contracts or rely on anyone else (a supplier, retailer, or attorney) to do so.

The UCC provides that where both parties are merchants and one party sends to the other a written confirmation of an oral contract within a reasonable time after that contract was made, and the recipient does not object to the confirming memorandum within ten days of its receipt, the contract will be deemed enforceable.

A *merchant* is defined as any person who normally deals in goods of the kind sold or who because of occupation represents herself or himself as having knowledge or skill peculiar to the practices or goods involved in the transaction.

It should be emphasized that the sole effect of the confirming memorandum is that neither party can use the Statute of Frauds as a defense, assuming that the recipient fails to object within ten days after receipt. The party sending the confirming memorandum must still prove that an oral contract was, in fact, made prior to or at the same time as the written confirmation. But once such proof is offered, neither party can raise the Statute of Frauds to avoid enforcement of agreement.

The advantage of the confirming memorandum over a written contract lies in the fact that the confirming memorandum can be used without the active participation of the other contracting party. It would suffice, for example, to simply state: "This memorandum is to confirm our oral agreement."

But since you would still have to prove the terms of that agreement, it would be useful to provide a bit more detail in the confirming memorandum, such as the subject of the contract, the date it was made and the price or other consideration to be paid. Thus you might draft something like the following:

> This memorandum is to confirm our oral agreement made on July 3, 1988 pursuant to which supplier agreed to deliver to purchaser on or before September 19, 1989, five thousand sheets of letterhead for the purchase price of $600.

The advantages of providing some detail in the confirming memorandum are twofold. First, in the event of a dispute, you could introduce the memorandum as proof of the terms of the oral agreement. And second, the recipient of the memorandum will be precluded from offering any proof regarding the terms of the oral contract that contradicts the terms contained in the memorandum. The recipient or, for that matter, the party sending the memorandum can introduce proof only regarding the terms of the oral contract that are consistent with the terms, if any, found in the memorandum. Thus, the purchaser in the above example would be precluded from claiming that the contract called for delivery of ten thousand sheets of letterhead because the quantity was stated in the written memo and not objected to.

On the other hand, the purchaser would be permitted to testify that the oral contract required the supplier to engrave the letterhead in a specific way since this testimony would not be inconsistent with the terms stated in the memorandum.

One party to a contract can prevent the other from adding or inventing terms that are not spelled out in the confirming memorandum by ending the memorandum with a clause requiring all other provisions to be contained in a written and signed document. Such a clause might read:

> This is the entire agreement between the parties and no modification, alteration, or additional terms shall be enforceable unless in writing and signed by both parties.

To sum up, business people should not rely on oral contracts alone since they offer little protection in the event of a dispute. The best protection is afforded by a written contract. It is a truism that oral contracts are not worth the paper they are written on. If drafting a complete written contract proves too burdensome or too costly, the business person should at least submit a memorandum in confirmation of the oral contract. That at least surpasses the initial barrier raised by the Statute of Frauds. Moreover, by recounting the terms in the memorandum, the business person is in a much better position later on to prove the oral contract.

Summary of Essentials to Put in Writing

A contract rarely need be—or should be—a long, complicated document written in legal jargon designed to provide a handsome income to lawyers. Indeed, a contract should be written in simple language that both parties can understand, and should spell out the terms of the agreement.

The contract would include (1) the date of the agreement; (2) identification of the two parties, the buyer and seller in the case of sale of goods or services; (3) a description of the goods or services sold; (4) price or other consideration; and (5) the signatures of the parties involved.

To supplement these basics, the agreement should spell out whatever other terms might be applicable: pricing arrangements, payment schedules, insurance coverage, consignment details, and so forth.

Finally, it should be noted that a written document that leaves out essential terms of the contract presents many of the same problems of proof and ambiguity as an oral contract. Contract terms should be well conceived, clearly drafted, "conspicuous" (i.e., not in tiny print that no one can read), and in plain English so everyone understands what the terms of the contract are.

7

Consignment

Many small-business owners are involved in consignment sales. Under a typical consignment arrangement, the consignor delivers an item to a dealer, or consignee. The consignee does not make an outright purchase of the goods but, rather, agrees to remit to the consignor the proceeds of sales less the consignment commission as the sales are made. Generally, the consignee is under no obligation to sell the goods and may return them to the consignor at any time.

Advantages of Consignment

Although it may not be immediately obvious, the consignment arrangement can be beneficial to both parties. For the consignee, consignments eliminate much of the financial risk of carrying goods of questionable market appeal. If the item does not sell, or sells poorly, the consignee will generally not lose much money since it has made no direct investment by purchasing the piece. The consignee only loses to the extent that the display space filled by the consigned work could have been filled by other items having greater sales potential, along with whatever amount of money was expended on advertising, overhead, etc.

The advantage to the consignor is that consignment provides an opportunity to get a product into retail outlets where it might not otherwise be accepted. Another advantage is that the consignor generally gets a larger share of the retail selling price—around 60 percent in consignment versus 50 percent in wholesaling. (That is changing, however, and consignment percentages are getting closer and closer to the 50 percent wholesale arrangement.)

Disadvantages of Consignment

But there are several deterrents which often make people reluctant to engage in consignment selling. After all, it is the consignor who takes most of the risks in such arrangements. Some of the questions that are bound to occur are: How promptly does the consignee pay after the product is sold? Is it insured while on the consignee's premises? Will unsold products be returned in good condition? And then there is all the paperwork and recordkeeping.

Other deterrents to the consignment arrangement are more complicated. What happens, for example, if a consignor delivers work to a consignee and the consignee then goes bankrupt? Or what if the consignee fails to pay debts to a creditor who has a security interest in all of the consignee's assets, including the consigned work? The resolution of these questions depends upon a determination of which party, the consignor on the one hand or the creditor or bankruptcy trustee on the other, has priority over the consigned work. There is no question that all of these parties may have valid claims to the work; the question is, rather, which claims are to be given first priority.

Your Situation in a Consignee's Bankruptcy

Before the enactment of the uniform state law called the Uniform Commercial Code (UCC) the consignor would generally prevail over the consignee's creditors or the consignee's trustee in bankruptcy with respect to the consigned item. Moreover, the consignor would prevail even though there was no record of the consignment that would give creditors or a trustee in bankruptcy notice of the consignment's existence. In effect, the consignor held a secret lien on the consigned work that was given priority over all other liens.

However, the UCC, which has now been enacted in every state except Louisiana, revised the rule of priority, largely in response to the general consensus that secret liens should not be legally enforceable.

Thus Article 2 of the UCC provides that where a consignor delivers work to a business dealing in goods of the kind consigned, the consignor will not have priority over the claims of creditors or a trustee in bankruptcy unless the consignor does one of three things:

1. Complies with the applicable state law providing that the consignor's interest be indicated by a sign on the goods, or
2. Establishes in court that the consignee is known by its creditors to be substantially engaged in selling goods under consignment, or
3. Complies with the filing requirements in Article 9 of the UCC.

As to the first option, most states do not have sign laws, and even in those states that do, the consignor should not rely on the consignee to place and maintain a sign on the goods indicating that they have been consigned, since it may not be in the interests of the consignee to do so. For example, a retailer would generally be in a much better position to obtain loans if a lending institution was led to believe that all of the work in the store was owned outright as opposed to being consigned.

Moreover, the consignor should not expect to prevail under the second option, since it will generally be difficult to prove that the consignee was known by the creditors to be substantially engaged in the business of selling consigned goods.

This leaves the third option. As a general rule, the consignor can best protect a consigned item by complying with the filing provisions contained in Article 9 of the UCC.

The purpose of the Article 9 filing requirement is simply to give notice to interested parties that certain property is subject to outstanding interests. The filing requirement gives notice to creditors, lending institutions and the like that the item in the retail outlet is subject to a consignment agreement between the retailer and the consignor.

That process is a complicated, time-consuming exercise that requires the filing of financial statements with the secretary of state in every state where the consigned goods are located, paying filing fees each time, giving notice to the consignee's creditors, and several other requirements.

There has been considerable debate as to whether the UCC provisions adequately safeguard the consignor's interests under consignment arrangements. As an initial consideration, there is the problem that the consignor may not even be aware that the protection exists. Many people who are just getting a business started are unaware of certain details of business and law such as consignor protection.

Moreover, even the consignor who knows the protection exists may be unable or unwilling to learn how that protection may be secured. Or, in the case of complying with the filing requirements of Article 9, many who know what is required may find that approach too complex and bothersome.

Special Situations

As a result of these problems and others, several states have enacted special artist-gallery consignment laws. The first of such laws was enacted by the state of New York in 1966. Thereafter, California, Connecticut, Massachusetts, Michigan, New Mexico, Oregon, Texas, Washington, and Wisconsin passed similar legislation. Other states are considering such laws, largely in response to increasing pressures from artists and arts organizations.

Although each state has enacted its own unique version, the basic provisions of artist-gallery consignment laws are essentially the same. Most statutes provide that any works of art delivered to any art dealer are presumed to be delivered under a consignment arrangement unless the artist has been paid in full on or before delivery. Thus the majority of transactions between artists and various art dealers will be deemed consignments for purposes of these statutes.

In addition, most artist-gallery consignment statutes provide that all consigned artwork, as well as the proceeds from the sale of that artwork, will be held in trust by the art dealer on behalf of the artist. This basically means that the art dealer will be solely responsible for any loss, theft, or damage occurring to the consigned artwork or the proceeds from the sales thereof that could have been avoided had the art dealer exercised the utmost care and caution. A few statutes go further by imposing *absolute liability* upon the art dealer for loss or damage, i.e., the art dealer will be liable for loss or damage to the consigned artwork even though such loss or damage could not have been avoided by the utmost care and caution.

Several of the new laws require the artist and dealer to enter into a written agreement containing at least the following information: the value of the artwork, the minimum price for which it can be sold, and the percentage to be paid to the dealer. Of course, the contract can contain more provisions, though an attempt to avoid the protective provisions of the consignment legislation is generally prohibited by the laws.

Finally, and perhaps most important, nearly all of these statutes provide that the consigned artwork is protected against all claims made by the art dealer's creditors, including the trustee in bankruptcy. Thus at least one effect of the consignment legislation is to provide artists with protection similar to that afforded by Article 9 of the UCC without requiring the artist to take any steps to procure that protection.

Craftwork: Covered or Not?

Although art-consignment legislation would seem to solve many of the practical problems with consignments of art, other business people should review how the applicable legislation, if any, defines the terms *art dealer* and *artwork*. Fortunately, an art dealer has been broadly defined by nearly all states as being any person engaged in the business of selling artwork other than a person exclusively engaged in the business of selling goods at public auction. On the other hand, artwork has sometimes been given a rather narrow definition. Some statutes have defined artwork as encompassing only the traditional areas of fine art such as painting, sculpture, drawing, and the like. This means that under some consignment statutes the product of the craftsperson may not be deemed to be within the purview of the statutory protection.

Other statutes expressly include as craftwork such items as those made of clay, fiber, wood, metal, plastic, or glass as being within the definition of a work of art protected by the legislation.

8

Collections

There are several ways to deal with collection problems, ranging from preventive action to initiating a lawsuit.

The general rule in a sales transaction is that payment is due upon delivery of the item being sold. While this rule may be subject to some technical complications that are beyond the scope of this discussion, it basically means that when work is delivered to a customer, the seller has the legal right to demand payment in full at that moment. This assumes that no arrangement has been made between the buyer and the seller that would allow the purchaser to delay payment.

While payment upon delivery is common in retail transactions, it is unusual when selling on consignment or in transactions between manufacturers and distributors. In addition, the purchase of a rather expensive item may be subject to an installment-payment arrangement.

If you are fortunate enough to deal with people who always pay their bills on time, the remaining portion of this chapter may be of no interest at all. However, if you have experienced delays in payment, or have had some totally uncollectible bills, you should consider the suggestions that follow.

Payment: After the Product Is Sold, or after an Invoice Is Submitted?

If you sell manufactured goods through a retailer, there are at least two possible payment arrangements. First, the goods may be consigned and payment is due only after an item is actually sold. Unfortunately, it is not uncommon for a retailer to neglect to inform a manufacturer of sales, or to delay notification for an unreasonably long period of time. When retail outlets are forced into bankruptcy, you can lose your consigned goods. This problem is discussed in detail in Chapter 7, which deals with consignment selling, with suggestions for protective steps that can be taken under the Uniform Commercial Code, especially in states where specific consignment-protection legislation does not exist.

The other method of payment is after you have submitted an invoice to the wholesale buyer. Commonly, invoices are payable within a specified time, usually thirty days after they have been tendered. This system virtually guarantees that you will not receive payment until the invoice is due. Indeed, unless some inducement for early payment is offered, you may wait interminably to be paid.

Ways of Encouraging Payment

Cash Discounts

A simple way to encourage early payment is by offering cash discounts. The offer of a 5 percent cash discount for early or even on-time payment may be all the encouragement some purchasers need. Some may ignore the appeal of a cash discount, however, if they are earning more interest on their cash reserves than is offered as a discount.

Charging Interest on Overdue Payments: Pros and Cons

The other option, which can be combined with the incentive of cash discounts, is to charge interest on payments received after the invoice due date. This method involves two possible traps. First, many states still have usury laws that limit the percent of interest that can be charged. A lender who exceeds the legal interest ceiling may find that the entire debt is forfeited, or all interest is forfeited, or that a usury penalty is imposed.

The second possible problem is the necessity to comply with the federal Truth-in-Lending Act and the various equivalent state laws. The Truth-in-Lending Act is basically a disclosure law which requires that certain terms be included on any contract or billing that charges interest. The required disclosures have been simplified recently and the task of compliance is further eased by the availability of pre-printed forms containing the required disclosures. While many of the required terms may seem inapplicable to a simple sales transaction, you are well advised, if you want to charge interest, to use a form that contains all the disclosures. These forms are available from legal publishers and private attorneys.

When the Payment Never Comes

If neither the carrot nor the stick is effective in obtaining payment, you have several other ways to go. The first possibility is to do nothing. If the amount is small enough, you may simply decide not to pursue collection. Needless to say, if this alternative is selected, you should refrain from doing any future business with that customer.

Lawsuit

A second option is the instigation of a full-scale lawsuit to force payment. In many states, a formal demand for payment must be made prior to commencing a lawsuit. Moreover, this option is only practical if the outstanding debt is relatively large, since an attorney must be hired and will likely be quite expensive, particularly if the case proceeds all the way to trial.

The court fees charged for filing a case can be rather high, ranging from $40 in some states and courts to over $150 in others. The defendant(s) (the debtor) must be personally served with court papers, which costs an additional $15 to $20 or more per defendant, depending on the difficulty of service. Lastly, if the case is won and the buyer still refuses to pay, further proceedings must be initiated at additional cost, to "execute," or force payment on the judgment received. All in all, on a moderate debt, the expense involved in a civil trial may amount to more than the debt itself.

Small Claims Court

A simpler and less expensive solution on small debts is to bring an action in small claims court. While the rules vary from state to state, all of the systems are geared toward making the process as swift, accessible, and inexpensive as possible. Moreover, most courts have staff members who help guide people through pleading in small claims court.

The major cost savings in a small claims court proceeding results from the fact that attorneys are not customarily permitted in such courts. Unless they represent themselves or a corporation, attorneys generally may not assist with completion of the necessary forms, or appear in court. Even in states where attorneys are not specifically barred by statute, the court rules are set up in such a clear, comprehensible way that an attorney is usually not needed.

A small claims action has other advantages over a conventional lawsuit. However, not all actions can be brought in small claims court. As the name implies, only claims for small amounts can be brought. The definition of *small* ranges from $500 in Arizona to $2,500 in Illinois. Moreover, only actions seeking monetary damages are appropriate in small claims court; other forms of relief, such as injunction, cannot be granted.

The small claims process is comparatively swift and inexpensive. Filing fees are generally under $35. In some states, such as Arizona, if the claim is extremely small (under $50), there is no filing fee at all. In addition, in most courts, the creditor is not responsible for informing the debtor that a suit has been brought. The clerk of the court customarily mails the notice to the defendant by certified or registered mail. A small fee is generally charged to cover mailing costs.

In many states, the hearing on a small claims action may be held on a weekend or in the evening. The hearing itself is kept simple. The technical rules of evidence and of legal procedure are not followed. The judge simply hears both sides of the case and allows any evidence or the testimony of any witnesses either party has to offer. Jury trials are never permitted in small claims court, although the defendant may be able to have the case moved to a conventional court if desiring a trial by jury.

An action in small claims court has disadvantages, too. First, the judgment is often absolutely binding, meaning neither party may appeal. Where appeal is allowed, as in New York State, the party wishing to challenge the judgment must show that a grave injustice has been done. This is not easy.

The other major disadvantage to a small claims action is that the judgment may be uncollectible. In many states the usual methods of enforcing a judgment—garnishment of wages or liens against property—are unavailable to the holder of a judgment from small claims court. In other states, such as New York, enforcement action can be taken only if the debt involved is the result of a business transaction and the debtor has three other small claims court judgments outstanding.

For the most part, care in selecting those with whom you do business will minimize the need to use legal means to collect payment for sales. However, if all other methods fail, small claims court is by far the least expensive and easiest way to obtain legal redress for a small outstanding debt. The drawbacks should be considered, however, before you decide to use it as a remedy.

Point-of-Sale Payments

Manufacturers who deal directly with the public at shows, fairs, or their own shops customarily expect to be paid at the moment they make the sale, before the item is taken away by the customer. Such payment is made by currency, check, or credit card. It is, therefore, necessary for you to determine whether the currency is authentic, whether the credit card will be honored, and whether the check is going to be honored by the bank. Obviously, the cash sale is the safest way, though you should be aware that counterfeiting is not a thing of the past.

Currency

Identifying counterfeit currency is usually very technical and difficult. Occasionally, however, it is simple if the counterfeiter has made a glaring error, such as using George Washington on a five-dollar bill. The federal government is quite diligent in alerting business people to the presence of counterfeit currency in a particular area when it is aware of the problem. The best way to avoid being stuck with a counterfeit bill is to keep your eyes open. It is a good idea not to accept any bill larger than $50.

Credit Cards

With regard to credit card fraud, the first thing to do is to compare the signature on the back of the card with the signature on the credit card slip. Even more important is to follow the credit card company's procedures carefully. If the company requires you to get authorization for all credit card sales over $50, then be sure to get that authorization. It may seem time-consuming and troublesome, but the rules are based on bitter experience. If you have made a credit card sale without following the instructions, and the credit card turns out to have been stolen or the buyer has exceeded his or her credit limit, you are likely to be stuck with the loss.

Personal Checks

The most frequent problems occur over personal checks. A host of things can prevent a check from being honored or cashed by a bank. To begin with, the person who writes the check may be an imposter, using a checkbook that actually belongs to someone else. In order to reduce the likelihood of this occurrence, you should insist upon seeing at least two pieces of identification, one of which should, ideally, contain a photograph of the person. A current credit card, or a check guarantee card with photo and signature facsimile are also good. Do not accept as identification such items as

Social Security cards, library cards, or any ID that can be easily obtained or forged.

Watch while the person signs the check (signatures may have been previously traced from a valid signature), and compare the signature with the signature on the other identification. While only an expert can identify a good forgery, clumsy attempts by amateurs may be easily recognized.

Accept checks only if they are made out to you and only if they are written for the exact amount of the sale. In other words, do not take checks made out to someone else and endorsed to you, never *cash* a check, and do not take checks for more than the sale amount —that is, when you then have to give change in cash.

Assuming that the individual writing the check is legitimate, there are still more potential problems. One of the most common difficulties is the problem of insufficient funds to cover the check. If the amount of your sale is substantial, it would be prudent to request a certified or bank-guaranteed check. However, the inconvenience of requiring the purchaser to have a check certified may interfere with impulse sales, and is thus not practical for many retailers.

If the person writing the check is known to you, it is less likely the person will give you a bad check. Even if the buyer is a stranger, the risk of receiving a bad check and not being able to locate the buyer afterward can be reduced if the buyer's address and phone number are copied onto the check from the supporting pieces of identification, if they are different from those printed on the face of the check.

Despite all these precautions, some bad checks do slip through. It is a crime in most states to pay for something with a check which the signer knows will be dishonored. A lawsuit can be brought against a buyer to recover the amount of the check. If you win such a suit, most states will allow the recovery of reasonable costs of litigation, including the attorney's fees.

A check returned for insufficient funds can be re-deposited in the hope that the check will be covered the second time through. Some bad checks are simply the result of a miscalculation of account balance or of the buyer having received a bad check. It is always a good idea to make a phone call before filing a lawsuit!

Bankruptcies

Straight Bankruptcy

There are two general categories of bankruptcy. The first, referred to as *straight bankruptcy* in Chapter 7 of the Bankruptcy Law, contemplates the prompt conversion of all of the bankrupt's non-exempt property to cash, and the payment of creditors to the extent possible. The Bankruptcy Law establishes a pecking order of creditors, giving some creditors priority for payment. Such creditors would be the U.S. government for taxes, and secured parties for the amount of their security interests. Each category of creditor must be paid in full before a lower-priority creditor may be paid at all. If there is not sufficient money to satisfy all creditors in a particular class, the members of that group will receive a *pro rata* portion of their claim.

There are some things among the bankrupt's assets that may be retained, such as a modest house, a holy book, clothing, and the like, even after bankruptcy. The list of exempt property varies from state to state.

After the bankrupt's non-exempt assets are completely distributed, the court-appointed trustee will apply to the bankruptcy judge for a discharge order. If the bankrupt has fulfilled all requirements of the Bankruptcy Law, and the judge is satisfied with the proceeding, then the bankrupt's debts will be wiped out—or *discharged*— and the proceeding will end. Certain claims, however, cannot be discharged in bankruptcy; for example, any creditor who was not notified of the bankruptcy and given a chance to participate in the proceeding will have a claim that remains viable even after the bankruptcy proceeding has ended.

Reorganization

The second type of bankruptcy proceeding is the so-called Chapter 11, or *reorganization*, contemplating a somewhat different process. Rather than terminating the business, a Chapter 11 is designed to facilitate an orderly payment to creditors so that the business may survive.

When the Chapter 11 petition is filed and the creditors meet, a reorganization plan is proposed. All legal proceedings for debt collection other than the bankruptcy proceeding are frozen, and the bankrupt is given an opportunity to satisfy the creditors in a timely fashion. Once a plan acceptable to all creditors is prepared, it is presented to the bankruptcy judge. If it is determined that the Chapter 11 reorganization plan is "fair and equitable," the judge will approve it and it will be implemented.

Creditors customarily receive more under Chapter 11 than they do under straight bankruptcy, although reorganization is feasible only for a healthy business suffering a temporary economic reversal. Creditors who have a secured position, such as those who have filed UCC documents to establish their security interest (discussed in Chapter 7), participate in drafting the Chapter 11 plan. Generally these creditors would be those who sold on consignment or those who retain a security interest for the purchase price of some goods. A plan will be deemed "fair and equitable" to the secured creditors, and they may be forced to agree to it, if it provides that they will:

Retain their liens and receive future cash payments equal to the value of the security; or

Retain a lien on the proceeds from the sale of their collateral; or

Receive the equivalent of their interests, such as cash up front or substituted collateral.

In a Chapter 11 proceeding, a secured creditor, in order to have the plan accepted by all the creditors, may be forced to accept a less favorable position than the Uniform Commercial Code would allow. Even though that may happen on occasion, someone with a security interest is still far better off than one who is unsecured.

Common sense, diligence, and attention to detail are always important attributes for any business person. When the economy is weak and money is tight, they become essential. There will probably always be some deadbeats and some uncollectible bills. But with proper care and some preventive attention, you can keep these to a minimum.

9

Franchising

Anyone who has successfully operated a small home-based business might wish to consider the opportunities available through a different form of business, the franchise. While fast food may spring to mind when you hear the word "franchise," this business form can be found today in virtually every line of product and service in the retail marketplace.

The purchaser of a franchise is basically buying a business whose method of operation has already proven successful. In fact, statistics suggest that 95 percent of new franchises succeed, compared to a 20 percent survival rate for other small businesses.

Where do you begin looking? Perhaps the best source for a complete list of franchise opportunities offered today is the *Franchise Opportunity Handbook*, which is published by the U.S. Department of Commerce and can be obtained from that agency. This handbook lists most registered franchise opportunities in the United States and gives a brief description of the nature of the business, the amount of the franchise fee, and information about the franchisor-franchisee relationship.

The Federal Trade Commission has adopted specific regulations for companies offering the sale of franchise opportunities. In addition, most states have adopted some sort of franchise regulation and approximately one-third of the states require franchise opportunities to be registered prior to sale.

A typical franchise statute defines a franchise as an agreement by which: (1) a franchisee is granted the right to engage in the business of offering, selling, or distributing goods or services under a marketing plan or system formulated by a franchisor; (2) the operation of the franchisee's business pursuant to such a plan or system is substantially associated with the franchisor's trademark, service mark, trade name, logo, advertising, or other commercial symbol designating a franchisor; and (3) the franchisee is required to give to the franchisor a payment or something of value (in legal terms, a valuable consideration) for the right to transact business in accordance with the marketing plan.

All companies that offer franchise opportunities are required to file with the appropriate regulatory agencies and to prepare extensive disclosure statements for publication in the Federal Trade Commission's "Uniform Offering Circular." By obtaining a copy of the "Uniform Offering Circular," those interested in a franchise will find a wealth of material including the following:

1. Information identifying the franchisor, its affiliates, and the affiliates' business experience since joining the franchise.
2. Information describing the business experience of each of the franchisor's officers, directors, and those management personnel responsible for franchise services, training, and other aspects of the franchise program.
3. A description of any lawsuits in which the franchisor and its officers, directors and management personnel have been involved.
4. Information about any previous bankruptcies in which the franchisor and its officers, directors and management personnel have been involved.
5. Information about the initial franchise fee and other initial payments that are required to obtain the franchise.
6. A description of the continuing payments franchisees are required to make after a franchise opens.
7. Information about any restrictions on the quality of goods and

services used in the franchise, where those goods and services can be purchased, and any restrictions requiring that purchases be made from the franchisor or its affiliates.

8. A description of any assistance available from the franchisor or its affiliates in financing the purchase of the franchise.

9. A list of restrictions on the goods or services franchisees are permitted to sell.

10. A description of any restrictions on the customers with whom franchisees may deal.

11. A description of any territorial protection that will be granted to the franchisee.

12. A list of the conditions under which the franchise may be repurchased or refused renewal by the franchisor, transferred to a third party by the franchisee, or terminated or modified by either party.

13. A description of the training programs provided to franchisees.

14. A statement regarding the involvement of any celebrities or public figures in the franchise.

15. A description of any assistance the franchisor will provide in selecting a site for the franchise.

16. Statistical information about the present number of franchises, the number of franchises projected for the future, the number of franchises terminated, the number the franchisor has decided not to renew, and the number repurchased in the past.

17. The financial statements of the franchisor.

18. A description of the extent to which franchisees must personally participate in the operation of a franchise.

19. A complete statement of the basis for any earnings claims made to the franchisee, including the percentage of existing franchises that have actually achieved the results that are claimed.

20. A list of the names and addresses of other franchisees.

After looking through the information in the offering circular, you should ask some hard questions about the opportunity. What sort of controls will the franchisor require of the franchisee with respect to sale of product, territory, etc.? What controls over advertising or promises regarding advertising does the franchisor make?

What is the financial condition of the franchisor; will it be able to deliver promised support? What earnings representations, if any, are made by the franchisor? Has the franchisor appropriately protected the trademark in the Federal Trademark Office and at the state level? What is the up-front franchise fee and will the franchisor expect, as is typical, a percentage of gross sales or continuing fees on an ongoing basis? Is the franchise for an indefinite term or must it be renewed on a periodic basis? What are the terms of renewal? Does the franchisor's system seem to be workable, understandable, and able to provide efficiencies necessary to justify the expense of paying a franchise fee?

Obviously, the checklist and tips could go on and on. It is quite clear that the purchase of a franchise ranks as a major lifetime investment. Before you make that investment, you should check out the pertinent information exhaustively and consult an attorney and CPA who have experience with franchises.

10

Multi-Level Marketing

A method of marketing which has gained popularity in recent years is known as multi-level marketing. The leading companies in this field have surpassed billion-dollar sales marks and their stock is traded on the New York Stock Exchange. Names like Amway, Mary Kay Cosmetics, and Shaklee are known in every household. Bob Hope touts their wares. Former Secretary of State Alexander Haig heads some of their international sales efforts. Prime-time television airs their commercials on a regular basis.

Analysts predict that this system of geometric growth will continue. Fortune 500 companies are eyeing this method of marketing for their own products. During the past few years, product lines have expanded dramatically. The corporations involved market everything from computers and video equipment to long-distance telephone service. Established companies appear to be thriving and new companies are proliferating at a fast pace.

What Is Multi-Level Marketing?

Simply stated, multi-level marketing is a form of marketing in which distributors or sales representatives sell products to the consumer in a one-on-one setting. In some cases, distributors purchase the company product at wholesale and profit from the difference between the retail and wholesale price. In other cases, a distributor really functions as a sales representative who takes orders for company products or services—for example, long-distance discount telephone services—and receives a commission for whatever is sold.

In all cases, distributors are entitled to sponsor other distributors or sales representatives and receive commissions on the sales of the sponsored reps as well as on the sales of any further representatives sponsored in a continuous "down line." For a successful distributor, the rewards can be substantial.

Any system that offers dramatic rewards and carries with it a low cost of entry obviously will tend to attract some of the best and some of the worst individuals. The system has not always thrived. Over the years, it has come perilously close to extinction as a result of prosecution by regulators who claimed the method promoted pyramid schemes under the guise of legitimate marketing. And, in many cases, the prosecutors were rightly chasing and eradicating unlawful pyramids.

Other programs which were in fact legitimate have survived. In a classic legal decision in 1979, the Amway Corporation prevailed in such a prosecution and in fact received a stamp of approval for its marketing program by the Federal Trade Commission. This particular decision opened the door to many other legitimate multi-level marketing companies.

Protective Regulations

Because of the abuses by the "rotten apples" of the industry, multi-level marketing has become a closely scrutinized marketing device. Regulations regarding multi-level marketing companies in the United States are a constantly changing patchwork of overlapping laws, which vary from state to state.

The basic thrust of these statutes is to prohibit marketing plans which require sales representatives to invest in the company or purchase the right to recruit others for economic gain. Under these statutes, multi-level marketing companies must be bona fide retail organizations which market bona fide products to the ultimate consumer. Inventory loading, such as requiring distributors to purchase a minimum amount of the product, and "headhunting," or remuneration for the mere act of recruiting others, are prohibited. Sales kits must be sold at actual company cost to sales representatives.

What to Look for

If you are considering work with an organization that makes use of multi-level marketing, you will want to be aware of the variety of abuses that have been targeted in leading legal decisions as potential elements of illegal marketing plans:

1. Products which have no "real world" marketplace;
2. Products which are sold at inflated prices;
3. Plans which result in inventory loading by distributors;
4. Substantial cash investment requirements;
5. Mandatory purchases of peripheral or accessory products or services;
6. Plans in which distributors are left with substantial unsold inventory upon cancellation of participation;
7. Plans in which fees are paid to distributors for headhunting and emphasis is on recruitment rather than the sale of product;
8. Misrepresentations or inflated representations of earnings.

In determining whether or not a program is a legitimate multi-level marketing opportunity, the would-be participant or the entrepreneur who is considering starting a multi-level marketing program should keep in mind several important points:

1. *Product.* The company should offer a high-quality product in which consumer satisfaction is guaranteed. It must have a demand in the marketplace. If the product is consumed by distributors themselves, it must be one that distributors would want to buy on its own merits, irrespective of participation in the marketing plan.

2. *Price.* The price of the product must be fair and competitive. Distributors should be able to purchase the product at wholesale or

at a substantial discount from prices found in retail stores.

3. *Investment Requirement*. There should be no investment requirement at all, except for a sales kit or demonstration materials sold at company cost.

4. *Purchase and Inventory Requirements*. A legitimate marketing program should have no minimum-purchase requirement nor any inventory requirement for someone to become or remain a qualified distributor or sales representative.

5. *Sales Commission*. Sales commissions should not be paid for the mere act of sponsoring other distributors.

6. *Buy-back Policy*. A legitimate multi-level marketing company will agree to buy back inventory and sales kit materials in resalable condition from distributors who cancel participation in the program.

7. *Retail Sales*. The focus of the marketing program should be to promote retail sales to nonparticipants.

8. *Distributor Activity*. Many of the statutes regarding multi-level distribution companies require that distributors perform a bona fide, supervisory, distributive selling or soliciting function in moving the product to the consumer.

9. *Earnings Statements*. The basic rule is that a legitimate marketing program should not make any earnings representations unless those statements are based on a verifiable track record of average earnings of distributors in a particular geographic area.

Multi-level marketing is clearly in a growth pattern. Its future course will require cooperation by companies, distributors, and those governmental agencies charged with regulating commerce to assure that legitimate practices prevail and pyramiding schemes are stamped out. Only history will tell whether our free-enterprise system has discovered a new and viable method of marketing.

11

Patent Law and
Trade-Secret Protection

Ordinarily, before a product can achieve a market edge, something must distinguish it from other items in the same general category. You will, of course, want to protect that "something" which sets your product apart so that others cannot exploit its uniqueness. Several bodies of law may help you obtain this protection. The copyright law, which is discussed in Chapter 13, grants to the creator of an original work of authorship which is reduced to tangible form, the right to prevent others from copying that work. Patent laws allow an inventor the right to prevent others from exploiting a patented invention. Generally speaking, a patent is available for any new and useful process, machine, method of manufacture, "composition of matter," or any new, useful improvement thereof.

As discussed in Chapter 13, copyright protection is not granted to items of utility. Thus, if a mason produces a decorative carved brick or block for use in an archway, no matter how beautiful, creative, original, or well executed, it is not likely to be protectable under the copyright laws of the United States.

Patent Protection

Such utilitarian objects may, however, be granted protection under the design-patent laws; for example, a particular sofa or chair may be design-patented, though only the aesthetic and not the utilitarian features are protectable. Similarly, a so-called mechanical patent, the one with which you are probably most familiar, may be obtained for any new and unique process, formula, or invention which is a substantial technological innovation. Unfortunately, patents are quite costly and difficult to obtain. It often takes an inordinate period of time for the patent document to be granted, and the period of protection is comparatively short (only seventeen years).

Another form of protection, known as the trade-secret law, allows exploitation of a particular innovation and may afford even greater protection than the copyright or patent laws. A trade secret may loosely be defined as anything which has not been revealed and could give you a competitive advantage. The secret should cover something which you actually use in your business and which you take some reasonable steps to protect. A trade secret may be lost if the owner fails to identify it or take reasonable steps to protect it. Otherwise, the trade-secret protection is perpetual.

The determination of whether patent or trade secret protection is most appropriate is sometimes referred to as the "patent or padlock dilemma." Indeed, it is not sensible to obtain both kinds of protection since achieving one will render the other meaningless. The patent-versus-padlock decision must be made within one year after discovery, since the patent laws provide that a patent can be obtained only when the invention in question has not been in public use for more than one year before application is made. Furthermore, use by the inventor for commercial purposes, even in secret, is considered a "public use" within the meaning of the patent law. Thus, during the first year, the inventor must decide how the innovation will be protected. If trade-secret protection is selected, then patent law is probably lost forever. Selecting a patent is also exclusive and will destroy trade-secret protection, since the patent application must contain a full description of precisely what was invented. *Letters patent*—the necessary documents—when issued, will cover what was disclosed. Thus, it is impossible both to get a patent and to keep some aspect of the invention secret. The patent application is not public information, however, and an applicant may withdraw the application at any time before letters patent are issued without destroying trade-secret status. In order to determine which of these methods of protection should be elected, you should consult an attorney who specializes in intellectual property. See Chapter 23, "How to Find a Lawyer and Accountant."

Trade-Secret Protection

All that is necessary for something to be protectable as a trade secret is that (1) it gives the possessor a competitive advantage; (2) it will, in fact, be treated as a secret by you; and (3) it is not generally known in your industry or business.

The fundamental question of trade-secret law is, What is protectable? The way you use knowledge and information, the specific portions of information you have grouped together, even the mere assembly of information itself may be a trade secret even if everything you consider important for your secret is publicly available information. For example, if there are numerous methods for producing a particular dye and you have selected one of them, the mere fact that you have selected this method may itself be a trade secret. The identity of your suppliers may be a trade secret, even if they are all listed in the yellow pages. The fact that you have done business with these people and found them to be reputable and responsive to you may make the list of their names a trade secret.

Many trade secrets will be embodied in some form of document. One of the first things you should do is to mark any paper, photograph, or the like, identifying it as confidential. You should also take steps to prevent demonstrations of your trade secret, such as manufacturing methods. Taking these steps will not create trade-secret protection, but the fact that an effort has been made to identify the materials and methods you consider secret will aid you should litigation ever occur. In this area, a little thought and cleverness will go a long way toward giving you the protection of the trade-secret laws.

First, you should have some degree of physical security. It has been said that physical security is 90 percent common sense and 10 percent true protection. You should restrict the access to the area in which the trade secret is used. Some precaution should be taken to prevent visitors from peering into the manufacturing area where the secret process, formula, or technique is employed. The credentials of delivery and service persons should be examined. The donning of a disguise to gain entry into a restricted area is a favorite ploy of business spies. Employee access to trade-secret information should be on a "need-to-know" basis; that is, employees should not be granted automatic free access to the material you desire to keep as a trade secret.

As noted above, documents containing trade secrets should be clearly labeled, as should pictures, sketches, and the like. A procedure should be established for controlled employee access to the documents. For instance, one person could be responsible for granting access to them, and a sign-in, sign-out process or the like could be instituted for those permitted access to the documents.

If possible, the information which you consider to be a trade secret should be fragmented. That is, no one employee should have possession of the entire secret; thus, no one person will have sufficient information to hurt you.

It is also a good idea to have employees sign a confidentiality and nondisclosure agreement when hired. An attorney who deals with intellectual property can prepare form agreements for use within your business.

If it ever becomes important for you to reveal a secret to an outsider, as, for example, when someone desires to purchase the right to exploit your innovation through a licensing arrangement, a different form of confidentiality agreement is in order. These agreements generally provide that in exchange for disclosure of the confidential trade-secret information, the party receiving such information will keep it in confidence and will not use it without the express written permission of the person making the disclosure. Again, your intellectual-property lawyer can prepare such an agreement for you.

Another method of protecting your trade secret is to engage in some vague labeling. For example, if your trade secret consists of a unique mixture for a glaze, then instead of having the components of the glaze bear their true names, you should label them "Ingredient A," "Ingredient B," "Ingredient C," etc. Then, if an employee quits, or if a stranger happens into your office, all they will learn is that by mixing some portion of A with some portion of B, combined with some portion of C, the desired result will be achieved. This will not be very useful information. Similarly, if the trade secret is the temperature at which a glaze is fired, instead of actually marking the thermometer you may wish to have the original temperature marks removed and replaced by colored zones.

If you are publishing in industry or trade journals, take care not to reveal trade secrets. Occasionally, manufacturers or their employees inadvertently disclose valuable information in an attempt to impress their colleagues.

In order to avoid the charge that you are stealing someone else's trade secret, you should question employees who come to work for you from a competitor. If there is any possibility of the new employee's using the competitor's trade-secret information, the new employee should meet with the former employer and get written permission to use the information while working for you.

Trade-secret laws may be the only protection available for your business secrets. Care should therefore be taken to restrict access to the information and to treat the information as truly secret. Contractual arrangements, both with employees and outsiders, are quite useful. These, coupled with your common sense in the day-to-day operation of your business, will go a long way toward protecting your intellectual property.

12

Trademarks

Many business people manufacture or market products which
they wish to have recognized as theirs. This is accomplished by
labeling the products with appropriate names, logos, or symbols
which are commonly known as trademarks.

Although modern trademark law is a relatively new development, its historical antecedents reach back to medieval England. In
those days certain craft guilds often required members to place their
individual marks on the products they produced so that, in the
event a product proved defective, the guild could trace its origins to
a particular craftsman and impose appropriate sanctions. Thus the
use of marks enabled the guild to maintain the integrity of its name.
Moreover, merchants would often affix marks to their products for
purposes of identification. Should the product be stolen or
misplaced, the merchant could prove ownership by reason of the
mark.

The use of marks for purposes of identification would no doubt
have worked quite well in an ideal society where all the citizens led
principled and moral lives. But such was not the case. Thus it is not
particularly surprising that unscrupulous merchants quickly realized that there was easy money to be made from the use of another's
mark, or one substantially similar. The shoddy merchants could

more readily sell their products by affixing to them the marks belong to quality manufacturers.

It was in response to this problem of consumer fraud that the first trademark laws developed in the United States. Initially the emphasis was on prevention of one person passing off his or her product as that of another. In contrast, modern American law focuses upon whether one mark is sufficiently similar to another to cause confusion in the minds of the buying public. The emphasis has thus shifted from the subjective intent of a dishonest manufacturer or merchant passing off goods as those of another to the objective determination of consumer confusion.

Yet, despite these changes, the essential purpose of trademarks and trademark laws has changed little since the days of the craft guilds. As discussed below, trademarks still function primarily as a means of identifying the source of a particular product. Moreover, trademark laws are designed to enable the trademark proprietor to develop good will for the product as well as to prevent another party from exploiting that good will—regardless of whether that exploitation is intentional or innocent.

The Need for a Recognizable Mark

What, exactly, is a trademark? A trademark may be defined as any word, name, symbol, device, or any combination thereof adopted and used by a manufacturer or merchant to identify one's own goods and distinguish them from those sold by others. The key concept is that the trademark must be *distinguishable*. In order to secure trademark protection, one must devise a distinctive mark.

The most distinctive marks are those that are purely arbitrary or fanciful, i.e., those that have no meaning or connotation other than identifying the source of a particular product. For example, the trademark *Kodak* to identify a brand of cameras is purely arbitrary. Less distinctive are trademarks having another meaning, such as the trademark *Shell* to identify gasoline. Although such trademarks as

Shell are not purely arbitrary, they are nevertheless afforded substantial protection since the other meaning bears no resemblance to the product identified.

Generic, Descriptive and Prohibited Trademarks

Generic and *descriptive* trademarks are not considered distinctive. A generic trademark merely identifies the product for what it is. Thus the use of the trademark *Beer* to identify beer is generic. Similarly, a descriptive mark merely characterizes the attributes or qualities of the product. For example, the trademark *Raisin Bran* to identify a cereal is descriptive since it simply describes the ingredients.

Generic marks are never afforded trademark protection. Descriptive trademarks, however, may be protected in limited circumstances. A descriptive mark may be protected if the proprietor of the mark can prove that it has acquired a *secondary meaning*. Secondary meaning will exist when the public no longer connects the words of the trademark with their literal, dictionary meaning, but rather with a unique product. For example, *TV Guide* has probably acquired a secondary meaning as the mark of a particular publication that contains television program listings and topical articles about the television industry.

In the Leathersmiths of London case in the mid-1980s, however, the question was whether the name Leathersmiths of London was a protected trademark. The court held that the word "leathersmith" is generic, at least when used to describe someone who is in the business of working with leather, and therefore is not entitled to trademark protection.

Some trademarks, even though considered distinctive, are nevertheless prohibited by statute or public policy. Thus obscene or scandalous trademarks are generally denied trademark protection. Similarly, trademarks that are deemed deceptive and misleading, such as the mark *Idaho potatoes* to identify potatoes produced in some area other than Idaho, are also denied protection.

Protecting a Trademark

In order to secure trademark protection it is not sufficient merely to adopt a distinctive trademark. The trademark must be *used*. A trademark is deemed to be used when it has been placed in any manner on the product or its containers or the displays associated with it or on any of the tags or labels affixed to the product. Thus it is not always necessary that the trademark actually be physically affixed to the goods. So long as the trademark is associated with the product at the point of sale and in such a way that the product can be readily identified as coming from a particular manufacturer or source, the trademark may be protected.

It should be noted, however, that the mere listing of a trademark in a catalogue, the ordering of labels bearing the trademark, the use of the trademark on invoices, or the exhibition of trademarked goods at a trade show may not be sufficient in and of themselves to constitute use, since the use of the trademark was not associated with the point of sale. To ensure trademark protection, the trademark proprietor would be well advised to physically affix the trademark to the product. In this way the product is certain to bear the trademark when it is sold.

Trademark Loss and Infringement

As pointed out above, use is a prerequisite to trademark protection. But some forms of use may result in the loss of a trademark. A number of well-known trademarks such as *Aspirin*, *Thermos*, and *Escalator* have been lost as a result of improper usage. Generally, trademark protection is lost because the mark is used in some capacity other than as an adjective modifying a noun. When a trademark is used as a noun or a verb, it no longer functions to identify the source of the product, but rather becomes the name of the product itself. At that point the mark becomes generic and not subject to protection.

Once the trademark has been adopted and used, it falls within the purview of common-law trademark protection. Common law protects the trademark proprietor against someone else subsequently using a trademark that is confusingly similar to that of the proprietor. (Common law is that body of law developed from court decisions rather than by state or federal statutes. Its advantage in this situation is that you do not need to take any action with any government agency to have protection for your trademark.)

This raises the question of when trademarks are considered to be confusingly similar. Generally, trademarks will be confusing if they are similar in sound or appearance, particularly if the trademarks are affixed to similar products or if products are marketed throughout the same or similar geographic areas. If, on the other hand, two products bearing similar trademarks are not related or are marketed in different geographic areas, there may not be any infringement.

Thus a business that distributes its products solely in the Northwest could probably adopt and use a trademark already used by a business distributing its product solely in the state of Maine, provided the mark of the Northwest business does not adversely affect the value of the trademark used by the Maine company. Moreover, a Northwest toy manufacturer could probably adopt and use a trademark used by a Northwest chainsaw manufacturer. In these situations there may be no infringement since it is not likely that the use of the mark by the toy manufacturer would confuse the chainsaw purchasers although, again, appropriation of another's trademark may be wrongful if the use, even by a noncompeting business, would dilute the value of the mark to the original owner.

When a trademark has been infringed, the trademark proprietor may sue the infringing party either for monetary damages or for an injunction prohibiting the infringing use, or sometimes for both. Monetary damages may be measured either by the plaintiff's losses resulting from the infringement or by the defendant's profits. In certain exceptional circumstances, where the defendant's conduct is willful and flagrant, the plaintiff might also be entitled to punitive or exemplary damages and/or attorney's fees.

Registering a Trademark

Thus far the discussion has revolved around the trademark protection afforded by common law. It should be observed, however, that the trademark proprietor may procure greater protection under federal and state statutes.

The federal statute governing trademarks is known as the Lanham Act. It is not the function of the Lanham Act to grant trademark rights (since those are secured by the common-law principles discussed above), but rather to provide a central clearinghouse for existing trademarks via registrations.

In order to obtain a federal registration of a trademark, you must first have a valid common-law trademark. That is, the trademark must be distinctive and be in use. In addition, the product to which the trademark is affixed must be sold, shipped or otherwise involved in interstate commerce. And, finally, as trademark proprietor, you must provide the Patent and Trademark Office with a written application, a drawing of the trademark in compliance with the rather detailed specifications of the trademark commissioner, five specimens or facsimiles of the trademark as it is actually affixed on or in connection with the goods, and a filing fee of $175.

If the examining officer at the Patent and Trademark Office accepts your application, the trademark will appear shortly thereafter in the *Official Gazette*. Any person may object to the proposed registration within thirty days after it has appeared in the *Official Gazette*. If nobody objects to the registration, or if the objections are found to be without merit, you, as trademark proprietor, will be issued a certificate of registration. At that point, you receive certain benefits and rights in addition to those afforded by common law.

Benefits of Registering

First, the registration enables the proprietor to use the symbol ® in conjunction with the trademark, which may well deter others from from using the mark. Second, registration is established evidence of the registrant's right to the exclusive use of the trademark. Finally, a registered trademark that has been in continuous use for a period of five consecutive years generally becomes uncontestable.

Thus, by registering the trademark, the proprietor may secure rights superior to those of a prior but unregistered user, but only if the original user does not object to the registrant's use within five years of registration.

A trademark registration remains in effect for a period of twenty years, and may be renewed in additional twenty-year increments by filing an application for renewal at least six months prior to the expiration of the existing twenty-year term.

Trademarks can also be registered under state law. The state trademark statutes generally grant rights similar to those of the Lanham Act except that those rights do not extend beyond the borders of the state.

In order to obtain trademark protection under state law, the trademark proprietor must file with the appropriate state officer a trademark application along with documentation similar to that required by the Lanham Act. The number of examples of the mark to be furnished may vary from state to state, and the registration fee may also be different.

Obviously, registration can be quite beneficial to a manufacturer who has invested a lot of time, money, and energy in developing a reputation for quality work. But procuring trademark protection on either the state or federal level may require a considerable amount of time and skill. In this regard an attorney may prove invaluable. An attorney can, first of all, determine whether the benefits to be derived from registration justify the expenses. (The total costs for trademark registration usually run about $500, not counting any artist's fees for drawings.) Second, an attorney can research a trademark index to determine if there are any conflicting marks. And finally, an attorney can complete the application and deal with any problems that may occur while it is being processed for registration.

If you are interested in contacting attorneys who specialize in trademark work, you can simply consult the yellow pages of the telephone directory (look under Patent Attorneys or Trademark Agents) or ask your state bar association for some recommendations.

13

Copyrights

It is quite common for start-up companies to use literature, computer software, videotapes, artwork and similar material created by others. This material may be protected by the copyright law, and its unauthorized use may subject the user to liability for copyright infringement. There are, however, some situations in which you may be able to use another's work without obtaining permission. The guidelines for this use are found in the federal copyright law.

Some businesses develop their own copyrightable brochures, catalogs, or the like, and since business people tend to take a proprietary view of their creations, they may wish to prevent others from using their work without permission. Again, the copyright law provides the vehicle by which these works may be protected.

In this chapter, I will discuss some significant portions of the copyright law and their possible application to you as a business person.

Copyright law in the United States has its foundations in the Constitution, which provides in Article I, Section 8 that Congress shall have the power "to promote the progress of science and useful arts, by securing for limited time to authors and inventors the exclusive right to their respective writings and discoveries." The first Congress exercised this power and enacted a copyright law. The legislation was periodically revised by later Congresses until 1909. No major changes were made in the law from 1909 until the Copyright Revision Act of 1976.

Prior to enactment of the 1976 law, unpublished works were protected by common-law copyright governed by state laws, which could vary considerably from state to state. Federal protection under the 1909 act began by protecting a pubished work to which a copyright notice was attached. The Copyright Revision Act of 1976 preempts the field of copyright law—in other words, it is now the only legislation generally governing copyright protection.

Publication within the context of copyright law is a technical term that applies to all copyrightable material. Under the old law it meant an unrestricted public display; today it means a *distribution of copies to the public*.

The new law became effective on January 1, 1978, but it is not retroactive. Thus, works created by the same person before and after January 1, 1978 will be covered by copyright laws that have some fundamentally different provisions. It is important to be aware of the basic differences and aware of which law applies to a given work.

Works created and sold prior to January 1, 1978 will be governed by the provisions of the old act. Works created but not publicly displayed or offered for sale prior to January 1, 1978 are governed by the new law. What difference does it make? In most cases, it will determine who owns the copyright in the work—the creator or the purchaser.

Ownership of Copyright

Under the old law, ownership of the common-law copyright in a work passed to the purchaser of that work unless the creator explicitly reserved the copyright in a written agreement. In other words, there was a presumption in the law that a sale included not only the work itself, but all rights in that work. Therefore, if you sold works before January 1, 1978 without reserving the common-law copyright, the copyright may now belong to the owners of those works as a matter of law. Two states, however, first New York, then California, recognized the unfairness of this and in 1968 and 1976, respectively, enacted legislation reversing this presumption. These state laws applied only to works sold in those states between the time of enactment and January 1, 1978, when the new federal statute went into effect.

The Copyright Revision Act of 1976 adopts the more liberal New York and California provisions by reversing the presumption that all rights are sold with the work. Today, unless there is a written agreement that transfers the copyright to the purchaser of a work covered by the copyright law, the creator retains the copyright. Ownership of the work is now recognized in federal law as separate and distinct from ownership of the copyright.

Works for Hire

An important exception to the copyright ownership rule is the classification of *works for hire*. In this classification, employers are granted the copyright in an employee's copyrightable work created within the scope of the employee's job. This is a rule that cannot be directly changed by contract, though employers can license or assign the copyrights they own. A license or assignment should be in writing specifying in detail the material that is to be licensed or assigned. In addition, a copyright, license, or assignment should be recorded with the copyright office.

A work for hire under both the old law and the new law is defined as "a work made by an employee within the scope of his or her employment." The principle has been based on several grounds: (1) the work is produced on behalf of and under the direction of the employer; (2) the employee is paid for the work; and (3) the employer, having paid all the costs and bearing all the risks of loss, should reap any gain.

The revised copyright statute recognizes a long-standing trade practice that the copyright of certain works created by independent contractors or by employees outside the scope of their employment belongs to the creator rather than the employer, unless the parties expressly agree in writing that the piece is to be considered a work for hire. Thus, a work specially ordered or commissioned is presumed *not* to be a work for hire if it is intended as

A contribution to a collective work,
A part of a motion picture or other audiovisual work,
A translation,
A supplementary work,
A compilation,
An instructional text,
A test or answer material for a test, or
An atlas.

In these instances, the creator is presumed to retain the copyright unless there is a signed, written agreement that the work will be considered a work for hire.

Joint Works

In a joint work, each contributor automatically acquires an individual ownership in the entire work. Section 201(a) of the Copyright Act provides, "The authors of a joint work are co-owners of copyright in the work." A *joint work* is defined as "a work prepared by two or more authors with the intention that their contributions be merged into inseparable or interdependent parts of a unitary whole" (17 U.S.C. Section 101).

According to the House Report the key point is the intention that the parts be absorbed or combined into an integrated unit at the time the work is created. The late Professor Melville Nimmer, of U.C.L.A. Law School, commented that although such an intent must exist at the time the work is created, not at a later date, the authors do not necessarily have to work together, work during the same period, or even know each other. However, the joint-works definition does not include the situation where an artist creates a work such as a piano solo, not intending that the work involve another artist, and later commissions lyrics.

Derivative Works

In the case of a *derivative work*, the contributing author owns only what that person contributed. A derivative work is defined (in 17 U.S.C. Section 101) as:

A work based upon one or more pre-existing works, such as translation, fictionalization, motion picture version, sound recording, art reproduction, abridgement, condensation, or any other form in which a work may be recast, transformed, or adapted. A work consisting of editorial revisions, annotations, elaborations, or other modifications which, as a whole, represent an original work of authorship, is a 'derivative work.'

Thus, any work based completely or substantially upon a pre-existing work, if it satisfies the originality requirement and is not itself an infringing work, will be separately copyrightable. The distinction between a derivative work and a joint work lies in the intent of each contributor at the time the contribution is created. If the work is created with the intention that each contribution be merged into inseparable or interdependent parts of a "unitary whole," then the merger creates a joint work. If such intention occurs only after the work has been created, then the merger results in a derivative or collective work.

Collective Works

A *collective work* is defined as: "A work, such as a periodical issue, anthology, or encyclopedia, in which a number of contributions, constituting separate and independent works in themselves, are assembled into a collective whole" (17 U.S.C. Section 101).

The originality involved in a collective work is the collection and assembling of pre-existing works, which are themselves capable of copyright, without any internal changes in such material. This assemblage of works is copyrightable.

Scope of Protection

What exactly is included in the "bundle of rights" that are protected by copyright? Five rights:

The right of first publication, which is the right to determine when and where your work will first be displayed to the general public or a substantial number of persons outside of family members and social acquaintances.

The right to control the first sale of the work. The only exception may be in cases where lienholders who were involved in producing or processing the work levy upon it for the satisfaction of unpaid debts.

The right to reproduce the work once it has been copyrighted.

The right to prepare derivative works based on the copyrighted work.

The right to display or to perform (where applicable) the copyrighted work publicly.

These rights are divisible, which means they can be transferred in whole or in part. If you take no special action when you sell a work, you will retain all the rights. You may, however, explicitly transfer a particular right if you wish.

The copyright law does not, in itself, provide economic benefits. It merely vests intangible rights in the owner, which allows the owner to bargain for future economic benefits such as royalties on reproductions.

Copyright Protection for Utilitarian Objects

Because copyright law was originally intended to protect literary works, earlier versions of the law omitted protection for three-dimensional designs. These designs were not given copyright protection until 1870.

The Copyright Act of 1909 did not contain any protection for utilitarian objects. But the regulations adopted to interpret the law extended copyright protection to the artistic elements of a utilitarian piece. The regulation stated that the aesthetic, but not mechanical or utilitarian, aspects of the item would be protected.

Despite the lack of specific legislation, some protection is available for manufacturers of utilitarian objects. The copyright law may be relied on to a limited extent. For example, if an individual draws a copyrightable picture and obtains copyright protection for that design, the copyrighted picture could be used or incorporated into any utilitarian item and be protected.

Originality Requirement

What is required to obtain copyright protection? The 1909 act specified that the work be both creative and original in order to qualify for copyright. The Copyright Revision Act of 1976 retained the requirement of originality although it only requires minimal creativity.

Originality is distinguished from uniqueness in that a work need not be unique, or the only one of its kind, to qualify for copyright protection.

For example, cartographers who independently create identical maps are each entitled to copyright protection. Because their works often look similar to the naked eye, many cartographers will include an intentional minor error on a map, so that if the identical error appears in another map alleged to be the original, the minor error will provide obvious evidence of copying. In writing this book, I have intentionally included typographical errors to inhibit copyright infringement.

Notice Requirement

The requirement that original works and all copies have the copyright notice affixed to them on publication is basic to both the 1909 Act and the Copyright Revision Act of 1976. The notice consists of the international symbol © or the word "copyright" or its abbreviation "Copr."; the name of the author (in the case of works for hire, this is usually the employer); and the year of first publication. For example:

Copyright 19__ by John Doe
or
© John Doe, 19__

The order of the words is unimportant.

Less conspicuous notice was permitted for artwork and other creations whose aesthetic value would be impaired by a large copyright notice. The standards were flexible but technical. If someone subsequently removed the copyright notice without permission of the copyright owner, this did not destroy the copyright protection.

Under the Copyright Act of 1909, a publication without notice caused the work to fall into the public domain and, once the rights were lost, they could not be retrieved. It was publication with notice that created a federal copyright under this law.

For example, the city of Chicago, in *Letters Edged in Black Press, Inc.* v. *Chicago*, lost the copyright on Picasso's sculpture "The Chicago Picasso" because a model of the work was placed on public exhibition at the Art Institute without a copyright notice attached, and photographs of the model, also without notice, were distributed to the press. The court ruled that the exhibition of the model (or maquette) without notice, as well as the distribution of photographs without notice, caused the work to fall into the public domain. The notice attached to the completed sculpture was invalid because this sculpture was, in the court's words, "a mere copy, albeit on a grand scale, of the maquette, a work already in public domain."

Under the Copyright Revision Act of 1976, a federal copyright is created as soon as an original work is made in tangible form. But the proper notice must still be attached at publication if you wish to retain a federal copyright after publication. However, a savings clause has been added in the new law; Section 405 provides that a copyright is not invalidated by publication without copyright notice under the following circumstances:

The notice is omitted from a small number of copies distributed to the public; or

The work is registered within five years of publication and a reasonable effort is made to add the notice to all works distributed in the United States after the omission is discovered; or

The notice was omitted, intentionally or otherwise, in violation of an express written agreement that distributed copies would bear the required notice.

This statute would change the result in a situation similar to "The Chicago Picasso" case, from January 2, 1978 on. Note that this statute is specifically designed to save copyrights when there has been an omission of copyright notice.

The Copyright Office has indicated that the savings provision of the law may not be used if there has been an intentional omission of the copyright notice by the person claiming copyright protection, though at least one case has allowed an individual to use the savings provision where there had been an intentional omission of the notice.

In addition, individuals who rely on the omission of notice when copying a work may be considered innocent infringers and, as such, subject to no damages.

Filing an Application and Depositing the Work

To register a copyright, you must *file* an application form with the Copyright Registrar, Library of Congress, Washington, D.C. 20559. You must also *deposit* two copies of the work. These are separate actions, although it is convenient to do them at the same time. Remember, if you have a copyright notice on your work, that means you already have a copyright. Under the Copyright Revision Act of 1976, registration is necessary *only* (1) as a prerequisite to commencing an infringement action; or (2) when the copyright owner wishes to take advantage of the savings provision of Section 405; or (3) if the Register of Copyrights demands registration of published works bearing a copyright notice (which is not likely to happen unless you have been in correspondence with that office).

The new law separates registration from the deposit requirements. Under the 1909 act, registration involved filing a copyright application, paying a $6 fee *and* depositing two copies of the work itself or two photographs of the original. However, fine prints came within the requirements of actual copies and thus it was necessary to deposit two actual prints. Congress recognized the economic hardship this caused artists, and the fact that many of them intentionally failed to take advantage of copyright protection because of the burdensome deposit requirement, and therefore modified it. Now the Registrar of Copyrights is allowed to exempt certain categories from the deposit requirement or provide for alternative forms of deposit. This has been done in the case of computer software, films, videotapes, and other items.

Under the present law, you should deposit two of the "best" copies of the work with the Library of Congress within three months of publication (creation). If the objects are bulky, fragile or valuable, photographs may be deposited instead of the actual work. The same photograph privilege applies to fine prints in editions of 300 or less. Filing the application (which incudes a $10 fee) need not be done when the two copies are deposited. When you feel depositing two copies is a hardship, you may apply for a waiver of the two-copy deposit requirement.

Although you can delay registration, there are at least two reasons why you should deposit the work and register the copyright (i.e., file the application) within three months of publication. The first reason is that the copyright law prohibits the awarding of attorney's fees and statutory damages for infringements that occur before registration, unless registration took place within three months of publication. The second reason is that if you deposit the required two copies of the work within three months but postpone sending the registration form and fee, the Copyright Office will require two more copies of the work when you eventually do send in the form and money.

Period of Protection

Copyrighted works under the 1909 act were protected for a period of twenty-eight years and could be protected for an additional twenty-eight, with the submission of an application for renewal. Under the revised law, works created on or after January 1, 1978 have copyright protection from the instant the work is fixed in tangible form until fifty years after the creator's death. This applies only to living persons. In other cases, for example a corporation that obtains a copyright in accordance with the doctrine of works for hire, the period of protection is either one hundred years from creation or seventy-five years from first publication, whichever expires first.

Infringement

The federal courts have exclusive jurisdiction over copyright infringement suits. Under both the 1909 and 1976 acts, the trial judge has wide discretion in setting damages. Under the 1909 act, a judge could award either actual damages (plaintiff's out-of-pocket losses or defendant's profit) or statutory damages. Under the 1976 act, a judge may also award actual damages, and the range of statutory damages is greater: as little as $100 for innocent infringement, between $250 and $10,000 for the normal case, and up to $50,000 for willful infringement. Both acts allow the awarding of reasonable attorney's fees to the prevailing party. Both acts also provide for injunctions against continued infringement and, in rare cases, impoundment. The statute of limitations for both acts allows a plaintiff three years to file a lawsuit after the infringement occurs. This time frame refers to the date the infringing was done, not when it was discovered.

In the case of willful infringement for commercial gain, criminal sanctions may also be imposed. The law was also modified in 1982 to provide more severe penalties for those who unlawfully reproduce and sell sound recordings, motion pictures, audio-visual works or phono-records. Under the new provisions, a criminal infringer may receive up to five years' imprisonment and/or a fine of up to $250,000.

Fair Use

In cases where someone is accused of copyright infringement, a major defense is *fair use*, a doctrine that was created and refined by the courts under the 1909 act. The 1976 act attempted to codify this judicial development and sets out four factors to guide courts in future applications of the fair-use doctrine. They are:

The purpose and character of the use, including whether such use is of a commercial nature or is for nonprofit educational purposes;

The nature of the copyrighted work;

The amount and substantiality of the portion used in relation to the copyrighted work as a whole; and

The effect of the use upon the potential market for or value of the copyrighted work. (Section 107)

The U.S. Supreme Court has interpreted this section of the copyright law in connection with motion pictures. In *Universal Studios, et al.* v. *Sony Corporation, et al.*, which the U.S. Supreme Court decided in 1984, the plaintiff movie producers claimed that the defendant, Sony Corporation, was enabling consumers to violate the plaintiff's copyright by selling a machine that could make off-the-air copies of the plaintiff's copyrighted works. This activity, it was alleged, should subject the defendants to liability for copyright infringement as both facilitator and conspirator.

The Supreme Court rejected this contention and held that the copying of copyrighted works in one's own home for non-commercial purposes was fair use, at least when applied to audiovisual works. The majority of the justices expressly refrained from considering the applicability of this doctrine to any other forms of copyrighted works. It is, therefore, unclear what the bounds of the fair-use doctrine are.

Congress is becoming involved in this area, and it is likely that legislation dealing with the boundaries of the fair-use doctrine will be forthcoming, though probably only as applied to audiovisual and perhaps audio works.

Getting Information and Forms

If you desire more information, write to the Copyright Office, Library of Congress, Washington, D.C. 20559, and ask for a free copyright information packet.

14

Licensing

Once you have obtained one or more forms of intellectual-property protection—a trademark, patent, or copyright—you may exploit your creations and prevent others from interfering with your rights. For instance, you may convert pictures from your copyrighted catalog into posters and sell them.

If another company likes your work and wishes to duplicate it, you can take advantage of your intellectual property by selling the other person a *license*.

A license to use your copyright, trademark or patent should be in writing. It should describe the scope of the user's permission: how long the license will last, whether the user can market copies throughout the world or only in specific locations, whether the license allows exploitation of the entire intellectual property or only a portion of it, i.e., use of a copyrighted photo on T-shirts only, and not on anything else, etc.

Method of Payment

Payment for the license should be spelled out in the license document. You can demand a flat fee in exchange for permission to use your copyrighted, trademarked, or patented object, or you may prefer to receive some portion of the income when the product is ultimately sold. This payment can either be fixed, for example, ten cents per item, or a percentage, perhaps 5 percent of the money received by the person exploiting the right. Care should be taken to define quite specifically the sum the percentage will be based on; specify, for example, if it will be a percentage of the gross receipts from the sale of copies of the copyrighted item.

Payments based on sales are referred to as *royalties* and you should be careful to define when they are due and payable. Unfortunately, numerous unscrupulous individuals have used "creative accounting" to reduce their obligations. In a California case, actor Fess Parker sued Walt Disney Studios to obtain an accounting for money he alleged he was owed for the Davy Crockett series. Parker apparently believed that the studio used an unusual method of determining his compensation.

It is also important to include in a licensing agreement a provision whereby you can verify the accuracy of the records showing what is due to you. This can be accomplished by requiring the person to whom the license was granted to have an accounting report preceding or accompanying any royalty checks. If you dispute the validity of the report, there should be an agreed-upon right to have an independent accountant audit the books. Some of my more confident clients have agreed to provisions which place the obligation for paying the outside accountant on the person who demands the audit only if an error of less than 10 percent of the total payment is discovered.

Acknowledgment of Copyright Owner; Quality of Reproductions

In order to retain the protection afforded by the patent, trademark, or copyright laws, you must require any person who uses your creation to acknowledge this fact and include the appropriate notice on the work. It is thus common to see a legend which states, "Reproduced with permission of J. Jones, the copyright owner."

Since the work marketed after you have granted a license will bear your name or trademark, it will usually be difficult, if not impossible, for consumers to distinguish between works reproduced by you and works reproduced by the person to whom you have granted a license. For this reason, it is important for you to retain some degree of quality control over the licensed product. A provision in the license should, therefore, require the licensee to demonstrate some method by which the item will be reproduced and some means by which you can evaluate the quality of the final products. To cite a grand example, when the Metropolitan Museum of Art in New York obtained the right to create copies of some of the pieces displayed in the King Tut exhibit, one of the primary concerns of the Egyptian government was the quality of the reproductions.

In order for the license to be valid and enforceable, it should be signed by both parties. You should make it clear that the license is personal and may not be assigned or exploited by anybody but the person to whom it is given, unless you give your written permission. It is also wise to provide that the license is void and no longer in effect if any of its terms, including payment of royalties or the like, are violated.

Lawyers who specialize in intellectual property can be helpful in explaining the myriad of options available to you through the licensing process. They can also be helpful in drafting a document which will afford you maximum protection while another person exploits your intellectual property. It is also important to record your license in the appropriate place: the Copyright Office or the office of the commissioner of patents and trademarks, when such recording is available. An intellectual-property lawyer should assist you with this process.

15

Warranty and Consumer-Protection Laws

Warranty Laws

You may be warranting certain attributes of your product whether you realize it or not. The rules that govern warranties have been embodied in the Uniform Commercial Code, which, as previously mentioned, has been adopted in all states except Louisiana and in most of the United States territories.

A warranty is in essence a guarantee that an item sold will be of a certain quality or have particular attributes. Giving a warranty involves certain obligations, so you need to be aware when you are doing so.

Any statement of fact or promise which describes an item will create an *express warranty*. In general, you do not need to use the words "warranty" or "guarantee" to create an express warranty. However, the more explicit your statement, the more likely it is that you, perhaps unwittingly, have given an express warranty.

Elements of an Express Warranty

In order to determine whether statements are the type which will give rise to an express warranty—as opposed to mere expressions of opinion, which will not—the courts have developed a test. If the seller makes a statement to the buyer relating to goods about which the buyer is uninformed, that statement is probably an express warranty. On the other hand, if the seller merely expresses a judgment about something on which each party would be expected to have an opinion, no express warranty is created.

For example, if a manufacturer were to state that a ceramic bowl was oven-safe, this statement would likely be considered an express warranty since most buyers do not know much about pottery in general, and only the seller would know about this bowl in particular. In order to determine whether a statement will be considered an express warranty, a number of factors are relevant. A written statement, particularly if it is part of a contract or bill of sale, is more likely to be considered an express warranty than an oral statement. How much the seller qualifies the statement is also an indication of whether an express warranty is created.

Another way an express warranty can be created is by giving a description of the item, which becomes part of the "basis of the bargain." The description does not need to be the sole inducement to purchase the goods in order for it to constitute a warranty. If a contract is involved, any statements must have been part of the contract negotiations, but the precise time a statement is made is irrelevant. The buyer could already have paid for an item and the seller could then make a statement which could be considered as part of the basis of the bargain since, theoretically, the buyer could still decide to return the goods to the seller and get the money back. However, these post-purchase statements must be made within a reasonable period of time to be considered part of the bargain and they probably only apply to face-to-face dealings.

An additional problem presents itself if you sell your goods both through a catalogue or ads and in person. Catalogs or ads and any statements made in them could be considered part of the basis of the bargain, although buyers would probably have to prove they relied on those statements in making the decision to purchase.

An express warranty can also be created by the use of samples or models. This type of warranty will arise if you sell from a catalogue or ship items from your stock after the buyer has viewed samples at a trade show. There is a distinction between a sample and a model. A sample is drawn from the actual goods which are the subject of the sale. Therefore, the sample describes the qualities of the goods being purchased unless the seller specifically states otherwise.

For example, if you show a customer one placemat from a group of eight and the customer does not investigate the other seven, an express warranty is created that the remaining seven are of similar color, size, and composition as the one looked at. A model, on the other hand, may not be drawn from the exact group of goods which are the subject of the sale. Therefore, a model is not quite as descriptive as a sample, but an express warranty can still be created.

Implied Warranties

In addition to express warranties, the Uniform Commercial Code imposes a number of *implied warranties*, presumed to be part of the sales transaction. One of these, the implied warranty of merchantability, applies whenever the seller is a merchant. Merchants are defined as people who deal with goods of the kind involved in the sale, or who, by their occupation, hold themselves out as having particular knowledge or skill. Merchants can also be those to whom this knowledge or skill can be attributed because they are acting as agents or intermediaries for a merchant.

Various tests for merchantability have been developed:

1. Does the item pass without objection in the trade under the description given in the contract between buyer and seller?
2. Is the item at least fit for the ordinary purposes for which such goods are used?
3. Does the item at least conform to any promises or affirmations of fact made on the container or label?
4. Is the item within fair, average quality of the description given?
5. Does the item run within the variations permitted by the agreement between the buyer and seller? Are the items of a con-

sistent kind, quality, and quantity within each unit and among units?

6. Is the item adequately contained, packaged, and labeled?

These are some, but not the only, tests of merchantability.

Note that to be merchantable an item need not be perfect. Trade usage, that is, the norms of a particular trade, will also establish the particular qualities which will be acceptable for items produced by members of that trade. Generally, the higher an item is priced, the more justifiable the buyer's expectations of high quality.

When a seller knows of a particular purpose for which the buyer is purchasing the goods and knows the buyer is relying on the seller's help to choose something suitable, there is an implied warranty that the goods will fit such a purpose. The usual way this warranty is created is when the buyer asks the seller for assistance. For example, if an individual comes to you and requests assistance in choosing a bedspread for a baby's crib, an implied warranty is created which would probably include at least two specific attributes: the bedspread is not made out of any toxic materials, so the baby can safely put it in her mouth, and it can be washed without running or shrinking, unless you specifically tell the buyer it must be dry-cleaned or hand-washed.

"A particular purpose" means a specific purpose for a specific buyer's use. Therefore, purchasing an item because it aesthetically pleases the buyer probably is not a particular purpose. It is an ordinary purpose. A particular purpose must be reasonably specific and explicit in order to assume that the seller has been informed of the buyer's purpose. In this regard, if the buyer is knowledgeable about what you sell, it is less likely that this implied warranty is created.

The one exception to this warranty is when a buyer asks for a particular brand or a particular company's product. In that case the buyer is not relying on the seller's skill and judgment, and no implied warranty is created.

A warranty of title is implied in every contract for sale of goods. It simply means that the seller has good title, or the right to sell the item, and that the seller is unaware of any outstanding lien against the item. The seller does not need to be a merchant as defined above and is not saved from liability by ignorance of a defect in the title. This warranty is based on the common-sense idea that the buyer should not have to defend ownership of goods against the claims of a third party.

The most modern of the implied warranties is the implied warranty against infringement. When an item is sold, the seller warrants that the item is not infringing any rights protected by patent, trademark, or copyright. Thus, if it appears that the object was created in violation of a third person's intellectual-property rights, the warranty is breached.

While there may at one time have been some technical legal defenses available to a defendant who, as a manufacturer, did not sell a defective item directly to an injured person, it appears that the vast majority of states would permit a victim to sue the retailer, wholesaler, manufacturer, or component-part manufacturer for injuries sustained as a result of a defective product.

Disclaimers

What can you do if you do not want to give one or more of these express or implied warranties? You can use a disclaimer, but it must be given in certain specific ways.

To be safe, disclaimers should be in writing. When you have given an express warranty, it is difficult to disclaim it. It is considered unreasonable to give an express warranty and then turn around and disclaim it. Therefore, *an attempt to disclaim an express warranty will usually not be effective*. If you describe an item, you cannot disclaim all express warranties in it and cannot limit the time period within which the buyer must discover any disclaimers contained in the warranty.

A common problem results when a customer claims that oral warranties were made before the signing of a written contract. The seller may be shielded from this problem by a rule which sometimes prevents prior oral statements from being considered as part of the contract. However, there are exceptions that you should be aware of. If there is a written agreement and it is not the final agreement, the written agreement will not supercede prior oral express warranties. Also, if the oral terms are consistent with a written disclaimer, they will be considered binding if the writing was not intended as a complete and exclusive statement of the terms. These types of problems tend to arise most often when someone else sells your goods for you. If you often have a salesperson sell your goods, you would be wise to include a limitation of the salesperson's authority on any written receipt.

Implied warranties can also be disclaimed. To exclude or modify the implied warranty of merchantability, the word "merchantability" must be specifically mentioned and the disclaimer must be conspicuous. This warranty can be disclaimed orally. But the implied warranty of fitness for a particular purpose can be disclaimed only in writing. The implied warranty of title can be disclaimed only by specific language or by circumstances which give the buyer reason to know that the seller does not have title or that the seller's title is subject to a third party's interest.

You are well advised to consult with an attorney to determine which warranties should be disclaimed and the best method of accomplishing this. The rules on disclaimers are quite technical and care must be taken in determining how much exposure you may have in a particular situation.

If you decide to give a written warranty or disclaim warranty protection in writing, you should be aware that there are federal regulations promulgated under the Magnuson-Moss Warranty Act to cover consumer products. According to the act, the following must be indicated in a written warranty:
1. To whom the warranty is extended;
2. Exactly what parts of the product are covered;
3. What the warrantor will do in case of defect;
4. When the warranty begins and ends;

5. What the buyer has to do to get warranty coverage;
6. Any limitations on the duration of implied warranties (this is not allowed in some states);
7. Any exclusions or limitations regarding relief.

In the written warranty you must also specify what you are promising regarding the material and workmanship and specify that the item is defect-free or will meet a specific level of performance. You must also clearly indicate whether the warranty is full or limited. Under a full warranty, the warrantor agrees:

1. To remedy the product within a reasonable period of time without charge if the product has a defect, malfunction, or fails to conform to the written warranty;
2. Not to impose a limitation on implied warranties;
3. Not to exclude or limit "consequential" damages unless this is clear on the face of the warranty; and
4. To replace the item or refund the purchase price if the item is unsuccessfully repaired numerous times.

If any one of the above qualifications is not met, you have given a limited warranty.

If you breach a warranty and the buyer is damaged by your failure to comply with the warranty obligations, the buyer may sue and you may be ordered to pay damages, court costs, and reasonable attorney's fees. Since this remedy exists, you should be careful to determine which warranties you are giving, and learn how to disclaim them if you do not want to give them.

Consumer Protection Laws

Cooling-off Period for Field Sales

The federal government and many states have enacted legislation designed to give consumers the opportunity to change their minds and cancel an unwanted sale. The federal law generally applies to any sale, loan, or rental of consumer goods or services which have a purchase price of $25 or more, in which the seller or the seller's representative personally solicits the sale, and the buyer's agreement or offer to purchase is made at a place other than the seller's place of business.

The "place of business of the seller" is defined as the main or permanent branch office or local address of the seller.

These laws protect the consumer by offering a cooling-off period within which to notify the seller of intention to cancel the purchase. The consumer may receive a return of all money paid and rescind any contract signed without further obligation. In effect, the consumer is given a period of time, typically up to midnight of the third business day following the sale, during which to determine whether he or she really wants to go through with the transaction.

The seller's principal obligation under these regulations is to disclose to the potential consumer that such a cooling-off period exists and that it is the consumer's right to take advantage of that escape clause and cancel the sale if desired. The form and content of this disclosure requirement is spelled out in the federal regulations.

To comply with the statute, a seller must be prepared to furnish the buyer with a fully completed receipt or copy of any agreement pertaining to the sale at the time the sale is made or the agreement is signed. The receipt or agreement must be in the same language which was principally used in the oral sales presentation. That is, if the presentation was made in Spanish, the receipt or agreement must also be in Spanish. It must also include the seller's name and address, time and date of sale, and a statement on the first page which contains the following language: "You, the buyer, may cancel this transaction at any time prior to midnight of the third business day after the date of this transaction. See the attached notice-of-cancellation form for an explanation of this right." The notice-of-cancellation form must detail the buyer's rights and obligations in the event the buyer chooses to cancel the sale.

In addition to the federal regulation, many states have enacted similar consumer protection statutes which provide for a cooling-off period and contain a similar disclosure requirement. Therefore, it is strongly advised that if you engage in sales other than from a permanently established business location, you confer with an attorney who can advise you of the legal requirements in your particular state.

Mail-Order Sales

Today, a popular method of selling is through a mail-order service or catalog sales. Here, too, the federal government has established certain guidelines aimed at protecting the consuming public. When a seller solicits a sale through the mail or through a mail-order catalog, the seller must reasonably expect to be able to ship any ordered merchandise to the buyer within the time stated in the solicitation, or within thirty days after receiving a properly-completed order, if no time period is stated. If the seller is unable to ship the merchandise within the specified time limit, the seller must offer the buyer the option either of consenting to a delay in shipping or of cancelling the order and receiving a prompt refund. The seller is also required to inform the buyer of any anticipated delays in shipping and to explain why the shipping deadline cannot be met.

Legal Advice Regarding Risks

You should consult with a business lawyer to evaluate the extent of exposure which may be expected as a result of the numerous warranties and consumer-protection laws which apply to sales. Warranty disclaimers and notices of right-of-cancellation, where appropriate, as well as limitations of liability can be used to reduce your exposure, but skilled drafting is necessary for effective protection. In addition, product liability insurance (next chapter) may be procured as a means of insulating yourself from extensive liability.

16

Product Liability

In November of 1978, a California jury awarded the victim of an automobile accident $120 million after his defectively designed Ford Pinto caught fire and exploded, inflicting serious personal injury. The size of this judgment against the Ford Motor Company staggered the nation.

Unless you happen to own a Pinto, you may ask, "What does this have to do with me?" The answer is that if you regularly sell a product, you might find yourself in court being sued by one of your customers for an injury if the customer claims that something you created was defective. The same laws that apply to the sale of a car by Ford apply to a sale by you. In one sense it seems quite logical and fair that the laws apply equally to all regardless of size. But when we look at the law, we see that it was not designed with the small business in mind.

History of the Liability Law

To understand the present state of liability law, it might be useful to briefly examine its roots.

In 1804 a craftsman named Seixas went to a warehouse to buy some brazilletto wood. I have never run across any myself, but the learned judge who wrote the legal opinion assured posterity that it was of considerable value. Woods, the warehouse man, sold Seixas some peachum wood instead, which is virtually worthless. Neither party, apparently, knew the difference between brazilletto and peachum.

When Seixas discovered the error he tried to return the worthless wood in exchange for either brazilletto or his money. The warehouse man refused because he had already given the money to the original owner of the wood. Seixas sued Woods and lost. He lost because even though Woods had written brazilletto on the invoice, he never warranted the wood as such and, besides, he did not know any more than the buyer did about different kinds of wood.

The result of this case can be amply summed up in the Latin maxim *caveat emptor*: let the buyer beware. This maxim was repeated time and again in both English and American cases until comparatively recent times. But now the pendulum has swung the other way and the rule has become *caveat vendor*: let the seller beware. The change came about gradually.

One of the harshest rules of early product-liability cases was that people injured by defective products could not sue the manufacturers unless they purchased directly from them. This technical requirement was carried down the distribution lines so that only individuals who dealt directly with each other had rights against each other, and consumers could not sue anyone but the retailers with whom they had traded.

This doctrine was recognized as harsh and formalistic; thus, it was not followed in a number of situations. For example, a seller, regardless of position in the chain of distribution, could be sued if negligent and if the product was "inherently dangerous." The courts struggled for some time over just what was and what was not inherently dangerous.

One early case said a car was not. But Supreme Court Justice Benjamin Cardozo, in a landmark decision, disagreed. To him a product was inherently dangerous if injury to the owner was predictable in cases where the item was defective. But almost anything can be injurious if defective, and so the decision holds today.

Where once a car was not deemed inherently dangerous, now negligence suits have been brought for such seemingly innocuous items as a toy top, rubber boots, and a lounge chair.

Cardozo made several other important pronouncements in the field of product liability. He stated, for example, that a manufacturer could be liable for defects in component parts made by another manufacturer if the assembler did not inspect them.

This shift of the burden of responsibility from the buyer to the seller is a natural response to several factors. First, as products became increasingly more complex, it was no longer true that the buyer and seller were equally knowledgeable or uninformed. Second, it was felt that businesses were large enough to bear the immediate losses and ultimately could spread the risk over a broad number of consumers. Since the majority of the products on today's market are mass-produced by large manufacturers, the rule reflects present economic reality.

Unfortunately, this is not the economic reality of the small business, and yet it too must learn to cope with these laws in a climate of litigious consumers and generous juries. It is better to learn about these problems while you still can protect yourself than when it is too late.

Product Liability

In every product-liability case the plaintiff must prove that (1) some injury occurred to the plaintiff; (2) the injury was caused by some defect in the product; (3) the defect was present in the product when the defendant had control over it. Once people get hold of your product you won't be able to stop them from injuring themselves, but you can control this third element by making sure that any item that leaves your control does not contain a defect.

There are two kinds of defects: mechanical defects such as loose screws, faulty component parts, and so on, and design defects such as instability, flammability, toxicity, tendency to shatter, and the like.

Liability for Mechanical Defects

Under the current rule of "strict liability" followed by a majority of the states, you can be held liable even for defects that could not have been discovered or prevented by human skill, knowledge, or foresight. Your only protection is insurance.

Many defects *are* detectable before an accident occurs if the right tests are made. And, following Cardozo's lead, the courts have held that manufacturers have a duty to inspect and test their goods. Failure to adequately test has been held reason enough to impose large awards of punitive damages on top of the actual damages awarded.

Tests and Records

How much testing is adequate? Sophisticated testing might prove to be too expensive for the small business. My advice is to design the best test you can for whatever you make, even if it is only a good tug here and there and, most importantly, to keep a record of it. This may serve to prove that you attempted to fulfill your duty to test the product. While this precaution might not protect you from product liability, it may result in reducing, if not eliminating, punitive-damage awards against you.

It is rare for an injured plaintiff to be able to prove that a defect was present when a product was purchased. The plaintiff frequently must rely on inferences drawn from the accident itself. If the jury is convinced that there is better than a fifty-fifty chance that the defect was there when the product was bought, the plaintiff will probably win. But if you come into court with a record of tests on your product, the odds might shift in your favor.

Besides keeping records of your tests, you should also keep records of your purchases of materials and devise some method of identifying the components in your product. That way, if you are sued for a defect in a component part, you can pass the liability on to the party really at fault. For example, if a stained-glass window collapses because the camming is inferior, you might be able to pass your liability on to the manufacturer of the defective cam.

Design Liability

The second category of defects, design defects, can be further subdivided: those that are and those that are not a violation of a statute. A 1959 case contains a good example of how far a court might go in defining a design defect. A rather obese woman entered a store and sat in a chair of contemporary design that the store had for sale. The back of the chair curved elegantly into the seat, which in turn curved down and around to form the base of the chair. It was along these serpentine curves that our overweight customer slid onto the floor. The injury to her pride was aggravated by an injury to her spine. The court held that the shape of the chair was defective, and awarded her $25,000 in damages.

In defective-design cases the courts have usually adhered to a common-sense criterion. If the product conformed to the state of the art when it was made, it will usually not be held defective. The state of the art is *not* the same as industrywide standards. Industrywide standards may be introduced in evidence, but it cannot be assumed that these assure due care. This is because the law will not allow an industry to adopt sloppy practices in order to save money or time when better, more protective methods are available. The state of the art, on the other hand, is the measure of how far technology in the field has advanced, and this will determine the norm for an industry.

In addition, a design may be defective if it does not meet the standards set forth in a statute. No product should be sold for consumer use before a check has been made to see whether it is covered by a consumer-protection law. A violation of these laws may carry criminal sanctions. In some jurisdictions, consumers injured by a product have proven their case by merely proving that a statute was violated in the production or sale of the product. The manufacturer would then have the burden of establishing that the injury was not the result of the statutory violation, which would be almost impossible in cases where the law had been enacted to prevent the very type of injury complained of.

Federal Laws

Not only is there state legislation pertaining to liability, there are at least three federal laws that directly affect the manufacturer. The first of these is a group of acts: the Hazardous Substance Labeling Act, as amended by the Child Protection Act of 1966, and the Child Protection and Toy Safety Act of 1969. These laws were passed in response to the staggering number of injuries and poisonings that occur to children under fifteen each year. They empower the Federal Trade Commission (the FTC) to name any potentially dangerous material a *hazardous substance*. Such substances may not be used in *any product* that might give a child access to the hazardous substance. That is, no amount of use or abuse by a child should make the product unsafe. Presently banned under this act are jaquitry beans used in necklaces, jewelry and dolls' eyes. For a list of other hazardous substances you should consult your local office of the FTC.

The second statute is the Flammable Fabrics Act. This statute empowers the FTC to establish appropriate standards of flammability for the fabrics used in clothing and household products, including children's toys.

Finally, there is the Consumer Product Safety Act, a statute that empowers the FTC to regulate the composition, content and design of any consumer product. The FTC has promulgated regulations for the use of architectural glass in doors, windows and walls and has banned the use of any surface-coating materials (paints) containing lead. This is a dynamic area, and all manufacturers should check with the FTC to determine whether the materials used in their products are subject to regulation.

The current law of product liability has held the seller of a product liable as well as the producer. A seller held liable for a defective product may in turn seek reimbursement from the manufacturer for the amount paid in damages. That may involve another expensive suit, and, if the manufacturer is broke, the seller is out of luck. There are two things that a seller might do for protection. First, incorporate. This business method is complex and is discussed in detail in Chapter 1. The second method of self-protection is to obtain insurance.

Liability Insurance

In general, the cost of liability insurance is affordable for the small business: $100,000 liability insurance for a person doing up to $10,000 of business a year will cost about $100 annually, although rates will vary from region to region. You should consult your insurance broker or agent to determine the rates in your particular area. You must then evaluate this cost against the risk of a law suit. Many product-liability suits are settled for, or are litigated to a judgment of, over $100,000. You can deduct the cost of this kind of insurance as a business expense for tax purposes. Given these factors, you should, if there is any reasonable expectation that a purchaser of your product could sustain personal injury from it, seriously consider obtaining product liability insurance.

Clearly, the area of product liability has evolved to a point where manufacturers are being held liable for injuries caused by their defective products. The doctrines appear to have evolved with an eye to the large manufacturer of a mass-produced item, but the rules are applied with the same vigor to the small manufacturer. It is therefore important to be aware of the potential risks involved and to take the necessary precautions.

17

Business Insurance

Today's insurance business originated in a London coffeehouse called Lloyd's sometime in the late seventeenth century. Lloyd's was a popular gathering place for seamen and merchants engaged in foreign trade. As Shakespeare pointed out in *The Merchant of Venice*, great profit can come from a successful sea voyage, but financial disaster can follow just as surely from a loss of ships at sea. From past experience, these merchants knew that despite their greatest precautions, such disaster could strike any one of them.

Through their dealings with the Italians, the merchants had become familiar with the notion of insurance, but there was no organized insurance company in England at that time. So when these merchants were together at Lloyd's, it became a custom to arrange for mutual insurance contracts. The method employed was for a ship's owner, before the ship embarked, to pass around a slip of paper that described the ship, its captain and crew, its destination, and the nature of the cargo. Those merchants who wished to be insurers of that particular ship would initial this slip and indicate the extent to which they could be held liable. This slip was circulated until the entire value of the ship and cargo was covered. This method of creating insurance contracts was called "underwriting."

Today, the term *underwriting* is used to describe the formation of any insurance contract regardless of the means employed in consummating it. Lloyd's of London still uses a method similar to that which originated in the coffeehouse, but most other insurance companies secure against loss out of their own financial holdings.

The risks covered by insurance, too, have changed. The original Lloyd's dealt in maritime insurance only. Now almost anything can be insured—from a pianist's hands to the Concorde jet.

Why Insurance for the Small Business?

Although your business may not be as perilous as was that of the seventeenth-century merchant, it is not altogether free of risks. Let me mention just a few of those risks.

Recent crime statistics show that even in rural areas you may become the victim of burglary. Various methods may be employed to protect against burglary, but none is perfect.

The forces of nature—fire, flood, earthquake—are undiscriminating in their targets. If you operate out of your home, you may already have homeowner's insurance against these, but you may find that your homeowner's insurance is inadequate to cover your supplies and inventory. In fact, your homeowner's insurance may not cover these at all, as will be shown later in this chapter.

A sale of your products subjects you to virtually unlimited liability to anyone who may be injured by one of them, no matter how careful you may have been in creating them. The potential magnitude of what this could cost you makes even the slightest chance of its occurrence a significant risk.

Loss of earnings through sickness or accident is a risk common to all small businesses. Some businesses that rely on a small number of partners for essential work may suffer a loss of earnings because of a loss of partners through sickness or accident. This risk is far too often overlooked.

Many risks can be insured against through any number of insurance companies. It should be noted, though, that there are some things that you *cannot* insure against. Insurance has a certain air of gambling to it. You put down some money and if a certain event occurs, you get back many times more. If it does not occur, you get back nothing. But that is where the similarity ends.

Public policy will not permit you to insure something unless you have what is called an *insurable interest*. To have an insurable interest, you must have a property right, a contract right, or a potential liability that would result in a real loss to you if a given event occurs. The reason behind this is simply to minimize the temptation to cause the calamity against which you are insured. History contains too many gruesome stories of desperate or crazy people obtaining insurance on a neighbor's barn or even a neighbor's child.

Of course, the requirement of an insurable interest has never stopped anyone from hastening that interest's demise or destruction. Recently, two businessmen were overheard at a party. One told the other that he had recovered one million dollars in fire insurance that year. The other businessman said he recovered *two* million for loss caused by a windstorm. The first, with greed in his eyes, asked, "How do you start a windstorm?"

The Basics of Insurance Law

Before analyzing the mechanics of choosing whether to insure a particular risk, I will briefly outline the law of insurance. All insurance is based on a contract between the insurer and the insured whereby the insurer assumes a specified risk for a fee called a *premium*. The insurance contract must contain at least the following: (1) a definition of whatever is being insured (the subject matter), (2) the nature of the risks insured against, (3) the maximum possible recovery, (4) the duration of the insurance, and (5) the due date and amount of the premiums. When the amount of recovery has been predetermined in the insurance contract, it is called a *valued* policy. An *unvalued* or *open* insurance policy covers the full value of property up to a specified policy limit. We will be discussing the advantages and disadvantages of each in this chapter.

The insurance contract does more than merely shift the risk from the insured to the insurance company. The insurance industry is regulated by state law so as to spread the risk among those subject to that same risk. The risk-spreading is accomplished by defining the method used for determining the amount of the premium to be paid by the insured. First, the insurance company obtains data on the actual loss sustained by a defined class within a given period of time. State law regulates just how the company may define the class. An insurance company may not, for example, separate white home owners and non-white home owners into different classes, but it may separate drivers with many accidents from drivers with few.

Next, the company divides the risk equally among the members of the class. Then the company adds a fee for administrative costs and profits. This amount is regulated from state to state. Finally, the premium is set for each individual in proportion to the likelihood that a loss will occur to him or to her.

Besides the method of determining premiums, state insurance laws usually specify the training necessary for agents and brokers, the amount of commission payable to them, and the kind of investments the insurance company may make with the premiums.

The very documents that a company uses to make insurance contracts are regulated from state to state. Sometimes the state requires a standard form from which the company may not deviate, especially for fire insurance. A growing number of states are stipulating that plain English must be used in all forms. Plain English is measured in reference to the average number of syllables per word and the average number of words per sentence. Because of a federal ruling that all insurance contracts are per se fraudulent if they exceed certain maximum averages, the insurance companies are forced to write contracts that an average person can understand. Nevertheless, only insomniacs read most insurance forms.

Expectations versus Reality

One frequent result of the gobbledygook that most insurance contracts are written in is that the signed contract may differ in some respect from what the agent may have led the insured person to expect. If you can prove that an agent actually lied, then the agent will be personally liable to you for the amount of promised coverage.

Most often the agent will not lie but will accidentally neglect to inform the insured of some detail. For instance, if you want insurance for transporting your products, the agent may sell you a policy that covers transport only in public carriers—when you intended to rent a truck and transport the products yourself. In most states the courts hold that it is the duty of the insured to read the policy before signing. If in the above example you neglect to read the clause that limits coverage to a public carrier you would be out of luck. Failure to read the policy is considered no excuse.

In other, more progressive, states this doctrine has been considered too harsh. These states will allow an insured to challenge specific provisions in the signed contract to the extent they do not conform to reasonable expectations resulting from promises that the agent made. In the example above it might be considered reasonable to expect that you would be insured when transporting your own goods. If the agent did not specifically bring your attention to this limitation in the contract, odds are that you would have a good case for getting rid of it.

Of course, I would not advise waiting for an agent to point out these unexpected variations even in the most liberal state. You should read the contract with the agent. If it is unintelligible, ask the agent to list on a separate sheet all the important aspects before signing, and keep that sheet.

Reforming the Contract

After the insurance contract has been signed, its terms can be *reformed* (revised) only to comply with the original agreement from which the written contract may somehow have deviated.

Let's consider the case of a woman who inherited a pearl necklace. An appraiser, apparently hoping for a large fee, misled her and told her the pearls were genuine and therefore worth $60,000. Before having them shipped from the estate, she obtained insurance on them in the amount of $60,000, paying a premium of $2,450. In the description of the subject matter it was stated that the pearls were genuine. The pearls were ruined after they arrived at the delivery terminal but before she received them. She tried to collect the $60,000.

In the course of the investigation of the accident it was discovered that the pearls were not genuine but cultured, and were worth only $61.50. Of course the insured could not collect $60,000 because no genuine pearls were lost or damaged. The worst of it was that she could not collect even $61.50 because the policy did not cover cultured pearls. The court emphasized that for reformation of the contract to be granted there must have been something either included or omitted contrary to the intention of both parties. In this case neither party ever intended to include cultured pearls, so the court refused to make a contract for the parties covering cultured pearls.

You might think that in this case the insured would get back her premium because there were never any genuine pearls to insure. She argued this but lost again. The court reasoned that had the pearls been lost in transit instead of being later destroyed, the actual value of the pearls would never have come to light. Therefore, the insurance company had indeed assumed the risk of paying out $60,000 and thus was entitled to the premium.

Overinsuring and Underinsuring

This case does not mean that if an insured accidentally overvalues the goods, no insurance will be recovered. Had the pearls been genuine but worth only $20,000 she would have recovered $20,000. Note that overinsurance does not entitle one to a recovery beyond the actual value of the goods insured. This is because one does not have an insurable interest beyond the actual value of an item. To allow a recovery greater than the value of the goods would be no different from allowing people to gamble with insurance policies.

Since you can at best break even with insurance, you might think it would be profitable to underinsure your goods. You could gain by paying lower premiums and lose only in the event that the damage exceeds the policy maximum. This has been tried and failed.

Let us study a case where the insured stated the value of her unscheduled property as $9,950 and obtained insurance on that amount. *Unscheduled property* means an undetermined collection of goods—for example, all a person's clothes and furniture—which may change from time to time. In this case, a fire occurred causing at least $9,950 damage. (See page 136 for more information on scheduling.)

The insurance company investigated the claim and determined that the insured owned at least $36,500 in unscheduled property. The company refused to pay on grounds that the insured obtained the insurance fraudulently. The court agreed with the insurance company, stating that the intentional failure to communicate the full value of the unscheduled property rendered the entire contract void. Therefore, the insured could not even collect the policy maximum. All she could hope for at best would simply be to get her premiums back.

Although at first glance this decision may seem harsh, its ultimate fairness becomes apparent with a little analysis. The chance of losing $9,950 out of $36,500 is greater than the chance of losing $9,950 out of $9,950 simply because most accidents or thefts do not result in total losses. In this case the insured should not have payed premiums for $9,950 coverage because she belonged in a much higher risk category.

Various tests are used by the courts to determine whether an omission or misstatement renders such a policy void. But in all cases, the omission or misstatement must be intentional or obviously reckless, and it must be material to the contract. Materiality is measured with reference to the degree of importance that the insurance company ascribes to the omitted or misstated fact. If stating the fact correctly would have significantly affected the conditions or premiums that the company would demand, then the fact is material. In the above case, had the full value of the unscheduled property been stated, the insurer would either have demanded that the full value be insured or that a higher premium be paid for the limited coverage. Thus, the misstatement was clearly material.

Unintentional Undervaluing

It should be noted that not all undervaluations will be material. Many insurance contracts do allow some undervaluation where it is unintentional. This provision is designed to protect the insured from inflation, which causes property to increase in replacement value before the policy's renewal date.

A so-called *coinsurance clause* generally provides that the insured may recover 100 percent of any loss up to the face value of the policy provided the property is insured for at least 80 percent of its full value. For example, if a house worth $100,000 was insured for $80,000 and suffered a $79,000 loss from a covered casualty, the insured would recover the full amount of the loss, or $79,000. If the property was only insured for $50,000, then a formula would be used to determine the amount of recovery. This formula is: divide the amount of insurance coverage by the total value of the property, and multiply the resulting fraction by the loss to get the recovery.

This gives us $50,000 (insurance) divided by $100,000 (value of building) times $79,000 (loss) = $39,500 (recovery). This example points out the importance of carrying insurance on at least 80 percent of the value of your property. Considering the inflation rate, it is wise to re-examine your coverage each year.

All insurance policies are limited to certain defined subject matter and to losses caused to that subject matter by certain defined risks. Once the risks are recognized, it is a simple matter to decide whether to insure against them or not. However, correctly defining the subject matter of insurance is tricky business. Mistakes here are not uncommon and can result in any one of us finding ourselves uninsured—like the woman with the pearl necklace.

Scheduling Property

The typical insurance policy will include various exclusions and exemptions. For example, most home-owner and auto-insurance policies cover personal property but exclude business property. If a manufacturer keeps certain products at home for personal enjoyment, are they personal or business property? The answer depends on whether the person ever sells or displays any of these goods. If any are sold or displayed, this may convert them all to business property.

In order to avoid the potentially tragic loss of such property, the manufacturer may schedule the pieces that are held for personal enjoyment. *Scheduling* is a form of inventorying where the insured submits a list and description of all pieces to be insured with an appraisal of their value. The insurer assumes the risk of loss of all scheduled works without concern as to whether they pertain to the business or not. Insurance on scheduled property is slightly more expensive than that of unscheduled property.

Many battles occur over the value of objects stolen, destroyed, or lost. In anticipation of such battles, you should maintain records of sales to establish the market price of goods and an inventory of all goods on hand. In the case of certain kinds of property (artwork, for example), the value must be determined by an expert in the field. However, this will not avoid all problems because the insurance company can always contest the scheduled value.

When and How to Insure

We now come to the most important issue: how to decide whether to insure and how to go about obtaining insurance.

Deciding Factors

Three factors should be weighed to determine whether or not to obtain insurance. First, you must set a value on that which is to be insured. Life and health are of the utmost value and should always be insured. Material goods are valued according to the cost of replacement. If you keep a large inventory of goods or if you own expensive equipment, it probably should be insured. The most elementary way to determine whether the value is sufficiently high to necessitate insurance is to rely on the pain factor: if it would hurt to lose it, insure it.

Second, you must estimate the chances that a given calamity will occur. An insurance broker can tell you what risks are prevalent in your line of work or in your neighborhood. You should supplement this information with your personal knowledge. For example, you may know that your workshop is virtually fireproof or that only a massive flood would cause any real damage. Although these facts should be weighed in your decision, you should not be guilty of audaciously tempting fate for, as the great tragedians have recounted, to scoff at disaster is to invite it. And if the odds are truly slim, but some risk is still present, the premium will be correspondingly smaller in most cases.

The third factor is the cost of the insurance. Bear in mind that insurance purchased to cover your business is tax-deductible. That means if you pay tax at a 30 percent rate, Uncle Sam is theoretically paying for 30 percent of your premium.

Keeping the Cost Down

As explained already, the premiums charged by an insurance company are determined by law. Nonetheless, it still pays to shop around. Insurance companies can compete by offering different packages of insurance and by hiring competent agents to assist you in your choice.

If there are enough small-business owners in your area engaged in a similar business of similar size, it may be possible for you to form a co-op insurance fund. To do this, you must estimate the total losses your co-op would sustain in the course of a year. Each member then contributes a pro rata share. The money is put into a bank to collect interest. If a disaster occurs and the losses are greater than the fund, each member must contribute to make up the difference. If there is money left over, it can be used to lessen the following year's premiums. This method is cheaper than conventional insurance because it eliminates insurance agents' commissions and whatever you would have paid toward the profit earned by the insurance company. But before you form your co-op, you should contact an attorney to determine what regulations exist in your state.

18

People Who Work For You

There comes a time in the life of almost every small business when it is necessary to get help, be it brain or brawn. The help most commonly needed first is the bookkeeper or accountant who can handle taxes, billing, and the like. When things get a little hectic around the shop or office, you might then hire someone to help with the packing or running errands. If selling is not your greatest talent, you may engage the services of a salesperson or a manufacturer's rep. And if this salesperson is really good, you will have to hire a helper to come in every day.

Independent Contractors

When you hire someone on a one-time or job-by-job basis, that person is called an *independent contractor*. Although you pay for their services, such people remain their own bosses and may even employ others to actually do the work for you.

If occasionally you give some of your work to a friend to sell on consignment, the friend would be an independent contractor. If once or twice a year you hire a bookkeeper or accountant to go over your business records, that person too is an independent contractor. The fact that the person is independent, and not your employee, means that you do not have to pay social security taxes in addition to the cost of the work, nor do you have to withhold income taxes or observe all sorts of other rules.

More important, if, while working for you, someone is injured as a result of the independent contractor's negligence, you will probably not be liable. However, there are situations where, despite your innocence, an independent contractor can render you legally responsible for his or her wrongful acts. Such situations fall into three basic categories:

• If an employer is careless in hiring an independent contractor and a careful investigation would have disclosed facts to indicate that the contractor was not qualified, the employer may be liable when the independent contractor fails to properly perform the job.

• If a job is so dangerous as to be characterized as "ultrahazardous" (a legal term) and is to be performed for the employer's benefit, then, regardless of who performs the work, the employer will remain legally responsible for any injuries that occur during the performance of the work. Thus, a fireworks displayer, for example, cannot escape liability by having fuses lit or rockets aimed by independent contractors.

• An employer may be required by law to perform certain tasks for the health and safety of the community.

These responsibilities are said to be non-delegable—that is, an employer cannot delegate them and thus escape liability for their improper performance. If, therefore, a non-delegable duty is performed by an independent contractor, the employer will remain responsible for any injury that results. A good example of a non-delegable duty is the law (common in many states) that home-owners are responsible for keeping their sidewalks free of dangerous obstacles. If a home-owner hires an independent contractor to fulfill this obligation by removing ice during the winter, the home-owner is still legally liable if someone is injured on the slippery sidewalk, even if the accident resulted from the contractor's carelessness.

Employees

The second capacity in which someone can work for you is as an *employee*. This category includes anyone over whose work you exercise direct control—helpers, apprentices, salespeople who represent you alone, a bookkeeper who is a full-time member of your staff, and so forth.

The formation of this relationship entails nothing more than an agreement on your side to hire someone and an agreement by that person to work. Although a written contract is not necessary except in the case of employment for more than one year, I suggest that employment terms be put down in writing, so that there is no misunderstanding later.

Employment Contracts

If the employment is to be for more than one year, there must be a written contract specifying the period of employment; otherwise, either party may terminate the relationship at any time.

While there is no prescribed form that the contract must take, there are nevertheless certain items that should be considered. The first item of an employment contract is the term of employment. An employment contract may be either terminable at will or for a fixed duration. Making the contract for a fixed period gives the employee some job security and creates a moral and contractual obligation for the employee to remain for the term. Of course, if the employee chooses to quit, or the employer chooses to fire the employee, the law will not compel fulfillment of the contract. That went out with selling orphans into apprenticeships and other forms of slavery.

The second item is the wage. Unless you are a large employer with forty-five or more employees, or are engaged in interstate commerce (which is defined as having gross sales of $500,000 or more), you will not have to comply with federal minimum-wage laws, but most states have their own minimum-wage laws. Other than the requirement imposed by this law, the amount of remuneration is open to bargaining.

In addition to an hourly wage or monthly salary, other benefits can be given, such as health and life insurance or retirement pensions. Some legal advice may be necessary here in order to take advantage of tax laws. In the event no salary is specified, the law will presume a reasonable wage for the work performed. Thus you cannot escape paying your employees fairly by not discussing the amount they will earn. If you hire a mechanic and the accepted salary in your region for a qualified mechanic is $20 per hour, then it will be presumed that the mechanic was hired for this amount unless you and that person have agreed to a different salary.

Third, it is often wise to spell out your employee's duties in the employment contract. This serves as a form of orientation for the employee and also may limit future conflicts over what is and what is not involved in the job.

Fourth, you may want your employee to agree not to work for someone else while working for you or, more importantly, not to compete against you at the end of the employment period. The latter agreement must be carefully drawn to be enforceable. Such an agreement must not be overly broad in the kind of work the employee may not do; it must cover a geographic area no broader than that in which you actually operate; and it must be for a reasonable duration—a five-year period has been upheld.

Finally, grounds for termination of the employment contract should be listed. Even if the contract is terminable at will, these grounds serve as useful benchmarks to guide your employee's actions.

Unlike the situation where you have hired an independent contractor, you are "vicariously liable" for the negligence and, sometimes, even the intentional wrongdoing of your employee when the employee is acting on your behalf. That means that if your employee is on the job and is involved in an automobile accident that is his or her fault, you as well as your employee are legally liable. It would be wise to be extremely careful when hiring, and to contact your insurance agent to obtain sufficient insurance coverage for your additional exposure.

Other Considerations in Hiring

There are other issues you should consider when hiring an employee, most of which fall into the realm of accounting or bookkeeping responsibilities. You should, therefore, consult with your accountant or bookkeeper regarding such items as the following:

1. A workmen's compensation policy for your employees in the event of on-the-job injury or occupational illness. State laws vary on the minimum number of employees which triggers this very important requirement. Many states' workers' compensation laws provide that an employer who has failed to obtain or keep in force required workers' compensation insurance will be absolutely liable, even in the absence of negligence, for on-the-job injury or illness, including not only medical expenses, but also damages for pain and suffering, lost earning potential, etc.

2. Withholding taxes: federal, state, and local. Here, too, the laws vary, and you must find out what is required in your locale.

3. Social Security (FICA). There are some exemptions from this body of social legislation. Contact your nearby Social Security office to determine how these exemptions may affect you.

4. Unemployment insurance, both federal and state. These also include certain technical requirements for subcontractors and the like.

5. Health and safety regulations, both federal and state.

6. Municipal taxes for specific programs such as schools or public transportation.

7. Employee benefits such as insurance coverage (medical, dental, legal), retirement benefits, memberships, parking, and so on.

8. Union requirements if you or your employees are subject to union contracts.

9. Wage and hour laws, both federal and state. These include

minimum-wage and overtime requirements. In some states the law also regulates holidays and vacations, as well as the method of paying employees during employment and upon termination.

As already noted, the requirements of these laws may vary dramatically from state to state, and you are well advised to discuss them with your lawyer, accountant, and bookkeeper. In addition, you should find out whether any other forms of employment legislation, such as licensing requirements, apply to you, your employees, or your business.

Hazards in the Workplace

On February 10, 1983, a sixty-one-year-old Polish-born employee of a film-recovery company in Chicago died of cyanide poisoning. He had worked for a small company which extracted silver from X-ray and photographic film. The work force consisted primarily of Polish and Mexican-American employees who spoke little English and were not very sophisticated. Many of the employees were not in this country legally.

To extract the silver, the film-recovery workers put the film in a vat containing cyanide and then transferred the film to a second vat which extracted the silver. The work was labor-intensive and the vats were not properly vented and emitted dangerous fumes. Many of the employees complained of symptoms associated with cyanide poisoning, such as dizziness, nausea, and a bitter taste in the mouth. The employer made no efforts to warn them of the hazards of the work.

After the employee died and was examined by a county medical officer, it was determined that the cause of death was cyanide poisoning. Government officials examined the plant where the employee had worked and found numerous health and safety violations. Eight months later, the president of the company and numerous corporate officials, as well as the company itself, were charged with and convicted of murder. The court concluded that the company, its officers, and directors were aware of the serious risk and hazards resulting from cyanide use, but they took no steps to alleviate the hazards in the plant. They did not even post warning signs that the foreign-born employees could understand.

While few manufacturers would intentionally injure a fellow human being, you may nevertheless find yourself in a similar situation. It is not uncommon to use toxic materials and to hire apprentices or employees in manufacturing. Often employees are not aware of the potential hazard which may result from the toxic materials. Unfortunately, few materials are labeled for toxicity.

It is advisable to research the potentially toxic effects of all substances used in your process or product, whether they are labelled for toxicity or not. You should then disclose to your employees at hiring pertinent information regarding hazardous substances.

Congress as well as federal administrative agencies is becoming more active in the field of regulation of hazardous substances. You should also be aware that your state workers' compensation agency or the Occupational Safety and Health Administration may have passed special rules regarding specific workplace substances and activities. It is critical to obtain a lawyer's opinion as to whether any of these regulations apply to your particular manufacturing process or other business. Your state's labor department may also be able to give you information regarding applicable workplace regulations.

Many manufacturers of art and craft supplies have begun to voluntarily label their materials with health and safety warnings. In response to pressure from art and craft advocate groups, the United States Congress in 1979 considered a federal law entitled the Federal Art Hazard Bill. After shuttling through several committees, it died in 1981.

Following the pattern established by the federal lobbyists, several states, including California and Oregon, recently enacted state art and craft labeling laws. Advocates of a healthy workplace are actively lobbying for similar laws throughout the United States.

Even though these laws are being enacted, your lawyer may not be able to tell you exactly to what extent you are legally obligated to advise your employees of potential risks inherent in their jobs. Again, the best course for an employer in doubt is to advise the newly hired individual of all known hazards which may result from the work and to disclose the fact that there may be other undiscovered risks in using the particular materials involved in creating the product. If an employment contract is used, a paragraph containing such a disclosure and the employee's acknowledgment of the known risks should be incorporated in the contract. A similar statement should also be included in any employment handbook.

While these documents would not provide a defense to a worker's compensation claim, they would sensitize employees to the need for caution in working with the toxic materials. Needless to say, you should take all precautions possible to protect the health and safety of your employees.

Termination of Employees

Determining if someone is an employee or an independent contractor is not always easy. The reason that the characterization is important is that employers are responsible for income tax withholding, social security, workers' compensation and the like, whereas one who merely hires an independent contractor is not.

There is another reason that the characterization may be important. If the individual working for you is merely an independent contractor, the contract between you and that person will govern your respective rights of termination. On the other hand, if the individual is an employee, care must be taken not to become responsible for a wrongful termination when dismissing the individual.

Historically, an employee who was not under contract could be terminated for any reason whatsoever. Approximately twenty-five years ago this right of absolute dismissal was challenged and the rule was modified. At that time it was held that an employee could be terminated for the right reason or for no reason at all, but could not be terminated for the wrong reason. Thus, an employee who was terminated for refusing to commit perjury before a legislative committee was entitled to recover against the employer for wrongful termination. The public policy in having individuals testify honestly was considered more important than the employer's right to control the employment relationship.

Recently, courts have become even more protective of the rights of employees. Thus, in a 1983 case (*Novosel v. Nationwide Insurance Company*) the United States Circuit Court of Appeals held that the power to hire and fire could not be used to dictate an employee's political activity, and that even a nongovernment entity is limited by the Constitution in its power to discharge an employee. The court, in essence, held that one's right to exercise constitutionally protected free speech was more important than the employer's right to control an employee's conduct.

Wrongful termination cases fall into three general categories. These include firing someone for (1) refusing to commit an unlawful act, such as committing perjury or refusing to participate in illegal price-fixing schemes; (2) performing a public obligation, such as serving on a jury or serving in a military reserve unit; and (3) exercising a statutory right, such as filing a claim for workers' compensation. Employers may not legally terminate an employee for the foregoing reasons. In a recent case the Arizona Supreme Court held that an employee who was terminated for refusing to "moon" fellow employees in a parody of the song "Moon River" during a company retreat was entitled to damage for wrongful termination. The public policy of protecting her right of privacy was deemed more important than the employer's right to terminate employees for disobedience. The courts appear to go quite far in holding that an employer cannot discharge an employee unless there is just cause for termination. A number of states have considered the adoption of legislation which would restrict the employer's right to terminate an employee to cases in which there was just cause. These laws also contain specific prohibitions on the termination of employees for "whistle-blowing," i.e., cases in which employees notify government authorities of wrongful acts by the employer, such as tax evasion, or cases in which employees tell corporate officers about wrongful acts of immediate supervisors.

Employers should take some precautions to avoid being placed in the untenable position of having bound themselves to individuals in their employment when the relationship has soured. This can result from language in employee handbooks, which might be construed as giving rise to a contractual right. It is also possible that oral statements made by recruiters or interviewers could give rise to contractual rights. To avoid this problem, an employer should have a legend placed in any employee handbook making it clear that the material is not an employment contract. It has also become common for employers to require prospective employees to sign a statement making it clear that the employment is at will and does not give rise to any contractual right. If there is a probationary period, the employer should be careful to state that the probationary employee will become a "regular" or "full-time" employee rather than a "permanent" employee. In addition, if there is any evaluation of the employee after the probationary period has ended, it should be conducted fairly. When evaluations become merely pro forma, problems can and do arise. Employees may argue that they have received sparkling evaluations and are being terminated for some invalid reason.

Perhaps an employer who uses evaluations should employ what has been characterized as progressive discipline. This procedure would be to start by orally warning a problem employee of your concern and progressively imposing disciplinary practices until termination becomes the only form of recourse left. Care should be taken not to violate the employee's rights since the liability for wrongful termination can be catastrophic to a small business. When in doubt, an employer should contact an attorney with some experience in the field of employment relations. In this area, as with many others, pre-problem counseling can prevent a good deal of time-consuming and costly litigation.

19

Keeping Taxes Low

Our income tax system is based on graduated rates. That is, individuals or organizations earning more money pay a higher percentage of tax. In other respects, however, large and small businesses are treated alike by the Internal Revenue Service.

Income Spreading

There are two important means of reducing tax liability. First is spreading taxable income by the use of several provisions in the tax code, and second is the use of deductions.

Income in Installments and Deferred Payments

One way a business can spread income is to receive payment in installments. Care must be taken with the mechanics of this arrangement, however. If a company sells a product for a negotiable note due in full at some future date or for some other deferred-payment obligation that is essentially equivalent to cash, or that has an ascertainable fair market value, the company may have to report the total proceeds of the sale as income realized when the note is received, not when the note is paid off with cash. However, the Internal Revenue Code enables a taxpayer who sells property with payments received in successive tax years to report the income on an installment basis. Under this method, tax is imposed only as payments are received.

For example, suppose you sell a custom-made computer software package for $3,000. Ordinarily the entire $3,000 would be taxable income in the year you received it. But if you use the installment method, with four payments of $750 plus interest received over four years, income from the sale will be taxed as the installments are received. In either case, the amount of income is $3,000, but under the installment method the amount is spread out over four years, and you are taking advantage of being in a lower tax bracket than had you taken the full $3,000 in the year you sold the software package. (However, be aware that if you sell real estate, there are special rules for installment sales; likewise, if you regularly sell personal property and are paid in installments, the amount you will be deemed to have received in the year of sale will be determined by a complex formula that takes into account your total amount of debt and the extent of your installment sales activity.)

Someone in a high tax bracket might wish to defer income until the future. For example, a commissioned salesperson could obtain an agreement from the employer that commissions paid would not exceed a certain amount in any one year, with the excess to be carried over and paid in the future. This would result in tax savings if, when the deferred amounts are finally paid, the salesperson were in a lower tax bracket.

There are drawbacks to deferred payments. These include the possibility that the party owing the money may not be willing to pay interest on the deferred sums, and the possibility that that party could go broke before the debt is fully paid. One should consider these risks carefully before entering into a contract for deferred payments, because it might be quite difficult to change the arrangement if the need should arise.

Spreading Income among Family Members

Another strategy for business owners in high tax brackets is to divert some income directly to members of their immediate families who are in lower tax brackets by hiring them as employees. Putting dependent children on the payroll can result in a substantial tax savings because the salaries can be deducted as a business expense, but at the same time you are not required to withhold social security from the children's wages.

Your child can earn up to the amount of the standard deduction without any tax liability. You as the taxpayer can still claim a personal-dependency exemption for the child if you provide over half of his or her support. This salary arrangement is permissible so long as the child is under nineteen years of age or, if over nineteen, is a full-time student. The child, however, may not claim a personal exemption if he or she can be claimed by the parents on their tax return.

There are other restrictions on such an arrangement:
1. The salary must be reasonable in relation to the child's age and the work performed;
2. The work performed must be a necessary service to the business; and
3. The work must actually be performed by the child.

A second method of transferring income to members of your family is the creation of a family partnership. Each partner receives an equal share of the over-all income, unless the partnership agreement provides otherwise. The income is taxed once as individual income to each partner. Thus, if you are the parent who heads a family business, you can break up and divert your income to your family members, so it will be taxed to them according to their respective tax brackets. The income received by children may be taxed at significantly lower rates, resulting in more income reaching the family than if it had all been received by the parent, who is presumably in a higher tax bracket than the children. But the law stipulates that if a child is under fourteen years of age, and receives unearned income from the partnership, any amount over $1,000 will be taxed at the parents' highest marginal rate.

Although the IRS recognizes family partnerships, it may subject them to close scrutiny to ensure that the partnership is not a sham. In addition, because partnership capital produces significant income and partners are reasonably compensated for services performed for the partnership, the IRS may opt to forbid the shift in income, in accordance with the Internal Revenue Code section which deals with distribution of partners' shares and family partnerships. The same section provides that a person owning a capital interest (or ownership interest) in a family partnership will be considered a partner for tax purposes even if he or she received the capital interest as a gift. But the gift must be genuine, and it should not be revocable.

Incorporating a Family

Some families have even incorporated. If the IRS questions the motivation for such an incorporation, the courts will examine the intent of the family members, and if the sole purpose of incorporating was tax avoidance, the scheme will not stand. If the IRS successfully contends that the corporation should be disregarded, the IRS can reallocate income from the corporation to the individual taxpayer. This will be done, for example, if the corporation does not engage in substantial business activity and does not observe corporate formalities, or if its separate status is not otherwise adhered to by the business person.

Tax Advantages and Disadvantages of Incorporation

A bona fide, or genuine, corporation, however, may provide some tax advantages for the small-business owner. As a corporate employee, the owner can control his or her taxable income with a limited salary, and part or all of the income the corporation receives from sales can be deferred. Although the corporation must recognize income whenever a sale is made, the corporation can deduct the owner's salary as well as other business expenses.

Nevertheless, incorporation is seldom advantageous for tax purposes. The Tax Reform Act of 1986 reduced individual rates so they are substantially in line with or lower than the corporate rates for most taxpayers. Additionally, there are some unavoidable legal and accounting expenses which will have to be paid by the corporation.

If your business operates on very small margins, you should determine whether the possible tax savings to you justify the additional cost of complying with the laws imposed on corporations. The cost to the corporation of payroll taxes, unemployment taxes, workers' compensation, and legal and accounting fees can be substantial. In addition, use of the corporate form is no longer necessary for setting up a retirement plan. Revisions to the rule for individual retirement accounts (IRAs) and Keogh plans allow a self-employed person to set aside as much money for retirement as could be done through a corporate retirement plan.

While incorporation may not provide tax benefits in some situations, and may even result in added expense, it still may afford you a liability shield. As I pointed out in Chapter 1, many businesses are incorporated for the sole purpose of obtaining limited liability for their owners, rather than for the tax treatment accorded corporations.

Moreover, there are several potential corporate tax problems the business person should consider carefully before incorporating. Making use of a corporate form means that any distribution of profits to shareholders in the form of dividends will be taxed twice: once at the corporate level as corporate income, and again at the shareholder level as personal income when profits are distributed to the shareholders (although there is a small dividend exclusion). Thus, although incorporation allows income to be shifted from the business person to other shareholders, such as family members, the shift occurs at the expense of double taxation. Obviously, it is important to consult with a CPA or tax advisor in order to determine whether the benefit of shifting income to a corporation outweighs the effects of double taxation.

Another alternative for the incorporated small enterprise is to organize as an S corporation. S corporation classification allows the owners to elect to be taxed much like a partnership and thus avoid double taxation. The Subchapter S Corporation is discussed under "Avoiding Double Taxation of Corporate Income" toward the end of Chapter 1.

Taxes on Accumulated Earnings and Passive Investment Income

If a person incorporates in order to postpone a significant portion of income, the IRS may impose an accumulated-earnings tax. However, the Internal Revenue Code (IRC) allows a maximum accumulation of $250,000 which is not subject to the accumulated-earnings tax, although for corporations whose principle work is in the fields of health, law, engineering, architecture, accounting, actuarial science, performing arts, or consulting, the maximum is $150,000. Accumulated earnings beyond these maximums must be justified as reasonable for the needs of the business. Otherwise, they will be subject to a tax of 27.5 percent for the first $100,000 of accumulated earnings and 38.5 percent for additional accumulated earnings in addition to the regular corporate tax.

The IRC also imposes an additional tax on most types of *passive investment income*, which is income retained by the corporation if the corporation is found to be a personal holding company. The rate for tax years beginning in 1987 is 38.5 percent, and for tax years beginning after 1987, 28 percent. This may occur if a majority of the corporation's income consists of copyright, book, movie, or other royalties; dividends; or personal-service contracts. But, if the owner sells his or her stock before the corporation has realized any income, the corporation could become a so-called *collapsible corporation*, causing the gain realized on the sale of the stock to be taxed at ordinary income rates.

Qualifying for Business Deductions

Up until now I have been discussing the various ways in which business owners can spread their taxable income or can take advantage of lower tax rates by incorporating. Another means of reducing tax liability involves making use of deductions. For this, you must keep full and accurate records. Receipts are a necessity. Even if your business is home-based, as are many start-up businesses, you should have a separate checking account and a complete set of books for all of the activities of your trade or business. A dilettante is not entitled to trade or business deductions, except against any income earned from that project.

Tax laws presume that a person is engaged in a business or trade, as opposed to a hobby, if a net profit results from the activity in question during three out of the five consecutive years ending with the taxable year in question. If the freelance writer, artist, craftperson, or the like, for instance, does not have three profitable years in the last five years of working as such, the IRS may contend that the work merely constitutes a hobby, in which case the taxpayer will have to prove *profit motive* in order to claim business expenses. Proof of profit motive does not require proof that a profit would actually be made; it requires proof only of intention to make a profit.

The Treasury Regulations call for an objective standard on the profit-motive issue, so statements of the taxpayer as to intent will not suffice as proof. The regulations list nine factors to be used in determining profit motive:

- The manner in which the taxpayer carries on the activity (i.e., effective business routines and bookeeping procedures);
- The expertise of the taxpayer or the taxpayer's advisors (i.e., study in an area, awards, prior publication, critical recognition, membership in professional organizations, etc.);
- The time and effort expended in carrying on the activity (i.e., at least several hours a day devoted to the activity, preferably on a regular basis);
- Expectation that business assets will increase in value;
- The success of the taxpayer in similar or related activities (i.e., past successes, even if prior to the relevant five-year period);
- History of income or losses with respect to the activity (i.e., increases in receipts from year to year unless losses vastly exceed receipts over a long period of time);
- The amount of occasional profits, if any, which are earned;
- Financial status (wealth sufficient to support a hobby would weigh against the profit motive);
- Elements of personal pleasure or recreation (i.e., if significant

traveling is involved and little work accomplished, the court may be suspicious of profit motive).

No single factor will determine the results. The case of *Deering* v. *Blair* provides an example of how the factors are used. Deering was the executor of the estate of Reginald Vanderbilt, whose financial affairs and residence were in New York. Vanderbilt had purchased a farm near Portsmouth, Rhode Island, because he was interested in horses, and operated it as a business. The business produced little income, but Vanderbilt claimed business expenses of over $25,000 in each of three years.

The court held that, despite the fact that he had several employees and advertised the farm's horse-boarding and rental services, the purpose for operating the farm was not to produce a profit. Rather, the land was used for pleasure, entertaining, exhibition, and social diversion.

The fact that Vanderbilt did not rely on the income from the farm for his livelihood was also considered by the court in making its decision. The business deduction was thus disallowed.

While a new business is not presumed to be "engaged in for profit" until it shows a profit three out of five years, deductions have been allowed even when this test is not met. In *Allen* v. *Commissioner*, the tax court decided that even though the ski lodge owned by the taxpayers and rented out during the ski season did not show a profit during the years in question, the lodge was operated as a business, so the deduction for expenses was allowed. The deduction was allowed even though the Allens did not depend on the income from the lodge for their livelihood. They did, however, keep accurate records, and did not use the lodge for their personal pleasure.

In *Engdahl* v. *Commissioner*, the tax court found a profit motive on the part of the taxpayers, who were considering retirement and wanted to supplement their income by operating a horse ranch. The court held that, despite a series of losses, the taxpayers had kept complete and accurate records reviewed by an accountant, had advertised the operation, took their horses to shows, and had worked up to fifty-five hours per week on the operation. Additionally, the assets of the ranch had appreciated in value. All of these facts showed that the taxpayers had a profit motive, and the business-expense deductions were allowed.

Once you have established yourself as engaged in a business, all your ordinary and necessary expenditures for that business are deductible business expenses. This would include materials and supplies, work space, office equipment, research or professional books and magazines, travel for business purposes, certain conference fees, any agent commissions, postage, legal fees, and accountant fees.

One of the most significant and problematic of these deductible expenses is the work-space deduction. It is not uncommon for smaller businesses to be based at home for a variety of reasons, the most important of which is probably economic. The cost of renting a separate office is such that many small-business owners, especially in the start-up phase, are unwilling or unable to pay for it. Others, of course, choose to work at home because it enables them to juggle work and family. Whatever the reason, taxpayers who wish to claim deductions for use of their homes in their business will have to do some careful planning.

Deductions for the Use of a Home in Business

For some time the IRS did not allow deductions for offices or studios in homes. This policy was challenged in a case in which a physician managed rental properties as a sideline. The doctor's rental business was run out of an office in his house, and the space was used only for this particular business. When the physician deducted the expenses for the office in his home, the IRS disallowed the deduction. But the court was apparently convinced by the physical set-up of the room that the doctor used it exclusively and regularly as an office in connection with his rental business. The court noted the room had no television set, sofa, or bed.

This decision now has been incorporated into the tax code. As a general rule, a business deduction is not allowed for the use of a dwelling that is used by the taxpayer during the taxable year as a residence. Use as a residence is defined as the use of the unit for personal purposes for more than fourteen days of the taxable year. But the Code makes an exception to this general rule in certain circumstances, allowing the taxpayer to take a deduction for a portion of a dwelling unit "exclusively used on a regular basis . . . as a principal place of business for any trade or business of the taxpayer," even if that business is not the taxpayer's primary source of income.

Exclusive and Regular Use

The exclusive and regular use exception applies to any portion of the residence used *exclusively* and *on a regular basis* as the owner's *principal place* of conducting that business.

The qualifications for this exception are strictly construed by the IRS and the courts. The requirement of exclusivity means that the taxpayer may not mix personal use and business use; in other words, an office that doubles as a storeroom for personal belongings, a laundry room, guest bedroom or the like will not qualify as an office for tax purposes, and a taxpayer may not deduct such space as an office.

However, there has been a recent liberalization of this rule in some parts of the country where the courts have held that a studio or an office can exist in a room that has a personal use, so long as a clearly defined area is used exclusively for business. It is important to remember that generally the Internal Revenue Service functions on a regional basis. Except for issues that have been reserved for decision by the National Office, each IRS office is independent and makes its own decisions until the United States Supreme Court or Congress makes a decision that applies nationally. That is why the decision by a circuit court in one area may not apply elsewhere.

The requirement regarding regular use means that the use of the room may not be merely incidental or occasional. Obviously, there is a gray area between regular and occasional. Perhaps some business owners just starting up can use this rule as an inducement to overcome temporary bouts of laziness or ennui. For if you are planning on deducting any expenses for your office, you must keep working to satisfy the regularity test.

Like the regularity requirement, the rule regarding the principal place of business has been very vague. However, under a proposed IRS regulation, a taxpayer may have a different principal place of business for each trade or business in which that person is engaged. The test requires looking at the particular facts of each case, but generally the key elements are (1) the amount of income derived from the business done there, (2) the amount of time spent there, and (3) the nature of the facility.

Thus it is now possible, for example, for a teacher, whose principal place of business (judging by income and time spent) is a school, to also run a sideline business of selling cosmetics out of the home and to claim the home office as the principal place of business for the cosmetics enterprise. A university professor who writes at home, on the other hand, may have a more difficult time qualifying for the office-at-home deduction. The difference is that although many professors prefer to write in offices at home, their writing is not a sideline or separate business as cosmetics would be for a teacher.

In *Meiers* v. *Commissioner*, the plaintiff owned a self-service laundromat. Mrs. Meiers managed the business, supervised the five part-time employees, and performed other managerial and book-keeping functions. She spent only about an hour a day at the laundromat, and two hours a day in her office at home. The office was used exclusively for activities related to business. The tax court ruled that since the laundromat was the "focal point" of the business, any deduction for an office in the home should be disallowed.

The Court of Appeals for the Seventh Circuit reversed that decision, holding that rather than using the focal point of the business as the basis of its decision, the tax court should have looked to the principal place of the taxpayer's activities. Managerial decisions were made from the office, and a conscious decision was made *not* to create an office at the laundromat itself. For these reasons, the office-at-home deduction was allowed.

In another case, the tax court disallowed a claim for an office-at-home deduction despite a unique argument. In *Baie* v. *Commissioner*, the taxpayers operated a hot-dog stand some distance from their home. Because the stand measured only 10 feet by 10 feet, some of the food preparation and storage was done at home. The ruling by the tax court was based on the fact that the kitchen and storage areas were not used exclusively for business purposes.

The taxpayers used the argument that they were actually engaged in a manufacturing operation at home, and therefore the office-at-home section of the IRS Code did not apply. The court held that the statute included such an operation, and the deduction was not allowed.

Another tax court decision denying the office-at-home deduction was *Moller* v. *United States*. The taxpayers were a husband and wife who claimed a deduction for the area of their home used to manage their investments. The court held that in order to qualify as a trade or business, the business must consist of the active buying and selling of securities, with income derived therefrom. The Mollers, however, derived their income from the dividends and interest resulting from holding securities for a long time. This, the court held, did not rise to the level of carrying on a trade or business.

When the office is in a structure separate from the principal residence, the requirements for deductibility are less stringent. The structure must be used exclusively and on a regular basis, just as an office in the home itself. However, when the office is in a separate structure, it need only be used "in connection with" the business, not as the principal place of business.

When taxpayers use a portion of their homes for storage of business materials (as well as for business), the requirements for deductibility of the storage area are also less stringent. The dwelling must be the sole fixed location of the business and the storage area must be used on a regular basis for the storage of the business equipment or products. The room used for storage need not be used entirely or exclusively for business, but there must be a "separately identifiable space suitable for storage" of the business-related materials.

Is the Office-at-Home Deduction Worthwhile?

If a taxpayer meets one of the tests outlined above, the next question is what tax benefits can result. The answer after close analysis is frequently, "Not very many." An *allocable portion* of mortgage interest and property taxes can be deducted against the business. These would be deductible anyway as itemized deductions. The advantage of deducting them against the business is that this reduces the business profit that is subject to self-employment taxes.

Of course, a taxpayer who lives in a rented house and otherwise qualifies for the office-at-home deductions may deduct a portion of the rent that would not otherwise be tax deductible.

The primary tax advantage comes from a deduction for an allocable portion of repairs, utility bills, and depreciation. Otherwise, these would not be deductible at all.

To arrive at the allocable portion, take the square footage of the space used for the business and divide that by the total square footage of the house. Multiply this fraction by your mortgage interest, property taxes, etc., for the amount to be deducted. How to determine the amount of allowable depreciation is too complex to discuss here, and you should discuss this with your accountant or tax advisor.

The total amount that can be deducted for an office or storage place in the home is artificially limited. To determine the amount that can be deducted, take the total amount of money earned in the business and subtract the allocable portion of mortgage interest and property taxes, and other deductions allocable to the business. The remainder is the maximum amount that you can deduct for the allocable portion of repairs, utilities, and depreciation. In other words, your total business deductions in this situation cannot be greater than your total business income minus all other business expenses. The office-at-home deduction, therefore, cannot be used to create a net loss. But disallowed losses can be carried forward indefinitely and deducted in future years against profits from the business.

Besides the obvious complexity of the rules and the mathematics, there are several other factors that limit the benefit of taking a deduction for a studio or office in the home. One of these is the partial loss of the *nonrecognition of gain* (tax-deferred) treatment that is otherwise allowed when a taxpayer sells a personal residence. Ordinarily, when someone sells a personal residence for profit, the tax on the gain is deferred if the seller purchases another personal residence of at least the same value within two years. Most of the tax on this gain is never paid during the taxpayer's lifetime.

This deferral of gain, however, is not allowed to the extent that the house was used in the business. This means that the taxpayer must pay tax on the allocable portion of the gain from the sale.

For example, if you have been claiming 20 percent of your home as a business deduction, when you sell the home you will enjoy a tax deferral on only 80 percent of the profit. The other 20 percent will be subject to tax because that 20 percent represents the sale of a business asset.

In essence, for the price of a current deduction you may be converting what is essentially a nonrecognition, or tax-deferred, asset into a trade or business property.

However, there is one important exception that can work to your advantage. The IRS has ruled that *if you stop qualifying* for the office-at-home tax deduction for at least one year before you sell the house, you are entitled to the entire gain as *rollover*, no matter how many years you have been taking the deduction. (A rollover means you can reinvest the proceeds of the sale in another dwelling within the prescribed period and avoid paying taxes.)

The word *qualifying* in the IRS ruling has a very important meaning. It does not mean only that you stop taking the business deduction for one year. It means that you physically move the business out of your home so that it no longer qualifies as an office at home, whether or not you take it as a tax deduction. The same ruling applies to the one-time tax exemption of up to $125,000 on the sale of a home by persons over age fifty-five. If you plan to sell your home any time soon, check all this out with an accountant or tax advisor. A little planning might save you a great deal of money.

Another concern is that by deducting for an office in the home, the taxpayer in effect puts a red flag on the tax return. Obviously, when the tax return expressly asks whether expenses are being deducted for an office in the home, the question is not being asked for purely academic reasons. Although only the IRS knows how much the answer to this question affects someone's chances of being audited, there is no doubt that a "yes" answer does increase the likelihood of an audit.

Given this increased possibility of audit, it doesn't pay to deduct for an office in the home in doubtful situations. Taxpayers who lose the deduction must pay back taxes plus interest or fight in court. One unfortunate taxpayer not only lost the deduction on a technicality, but also lost the rollover treatment on the sale of his home.

If you believe that your office at home could qualify for the the business deduction, you would be well advised to consult with a competent tax expert who can assist in calculating the deduction.

Other Professional Expenses

As mentioned earlier, deductible business expenses include not only the work space, but all the ordinary and necessary expenditures involved in the business. So-called *current expenses*, items with a useful life of less than one year, are fully deductible in the year incurred. Writing utensils and stationery, postage, and telephone bills are all examples of current expenses.

Many expenses, however, cannot be fully deducted in the year of purchase but must be depreciated. These kinds of costs are called *capital expenditures*. For example, the cost of equipment such as a typewriter, computer, word processor, or pickup truck, all of which have useful lives of more than one year, are capital expenditures and cannot be fully deducted in the year of purchase. Instead, the taxpayer must depreciate, or allocate, the cost of the item over the estimated useful life of the asset. Although the actual useful life of professional equipment will vary, fixed periods have been established in the Code over which depreciation may be deducted.

In some cases it may be difficult to decide whether an expense is a capital expenditure or a current expense. Repairs to machinery are one example. If you spend $200 repairing your delivery van, this expense may or may not constitute a capital expenditure. The general test is whether the amount spent restoring the vehicle adds to its value or substantially prolongs its useful life. Since the cost of replacing short-lived parts of a vehicle to keep it in efficient working condition does not substantially add to its useful life, such a cost would be a current cost and would be deductible. The cost of rebuilding your van's engine, on the other hand, significantly extends its useful life. Thus, such a cost is a capital expenditure and must be depreciated.

For many small businesses, an immediate deduction can be taken when equipment is purchased. Up to $10,000 of such purchases may be "expensed" each year and need not be depreciated at all.

Commissions paid to salespeople, as well as fees paid to lawyers or accountants for business purposes, are generally deductible as current expenses. The same is true of salaries paid to others whose services are necessary for the business. If you need to hire help, it is a good idea to hire people on an individual-project basis as independent contractors rather than as regular employees. This avoids your having to pay social security, disability, and withholding-tax payments on their account. You should specify the job-by-job basis of the assignments, detail when each project is to be completed and, if possible, allow the person you are hiring to choose the place to do the work.

Travel Expenses

On a business trip, whether within the U.S. or abroad, your ordinary and necessary expenses, including travel and lodging, may be 100 percent deductible if your travel is solely for business purposes, except for "luxury water travel." Business meals and meals consumed while on a business trip are deductible up to 80 percent of the actual cost. If the trip primarily involves a personal vacation, you can deduct business-related expenses at the destination, but you may not deduct the transportation costs.

If the trip is primarily for business, but part of the time is given to a personal vacation, you must indicate which expenses are for business and which for pleasure. This is *not* true in the case of foreign trips if one of the following exceptions applies:

You had no control over arranging the trip,

The trip outside of the U.S. was for a week or less,

You are not a managing executive or shareholder of the company that employed you.

If you are claiming one of these exceptions you should be careful to have supporting documentation. If you cannot take advantage of one of the exceptions, you must allocate expenses for the trip abroad according to the percentage of the trip devoted to business as opposed to vacation.

The definition of what constitutes "a business stay" can be very helpful to the taxpayer in determining a trip's deductibility. Travel days, including the day of departure and the day of return, count as business days if travel outside the U.S. is for more than seven days and business activities occurred on such days. Any day which the taxpayer spends on business counts as a business day even if only a part of the day is spent on business. A day in which business is canceled through no fault of the taxpayer counts as a business day. Saturdays, Sundays, and holidays count as business days even though no business is conducted, provided that business is conducted on the Friday before and the Monday after the weekend, or on one day on either side of the holiday.

Entertainment Expenses

Entertainment expenses incurred for the purpose of developing an existing business are also deductible in the amount of 80 percent of actual cost. However, you must be especially careful about recording entertainment expenses. You should record in your logbook the amount, date, place, type of entertainment, business purpose, substance of the discussion, the participants in the discussion, and the business relationship of the parties who are being entertained. Keep receipts for any expenses over $25. You should also keep in mind the new stipulation in the Tax Code which disallows deductibility for expenses which are "lavish or extravagant under the circumstances." No guidelines have yet been developed as to the definition of the term "lavish or extravagant," but one should be aware of the restriction nevertheless. If tickets to a sporting, cultural, or other entertainment event are purchased, only the face value of the ticket is allowed as a deduction. If a skybox or other luxury box seat is purchased or leased and is used for business entertaining, the maximum deduction now allowed is the cost of a non-luxury box seat.

Expenses That the IRS Scrutinizes

The above rules cover business travel and entertainment expenses both inside and outside of the United States. The rules are more stringent for expenses incurred while attending conventions and conferences outside the United States. Also, the IRS tends to review very carefully any deductions for attendance at business seminars that also involve a family vacation, whether inside the U.S. or abroad. In order to deduct the business expense, the taxpayer must be able to show, with documents, that the reason for attending the meeting was to promote production of income. Normally, for a spouse's expenses to be deductible, the spouse's presence must be required by the employer. In the case of an independent consultant who has organized into a partnership or small corporation, it is wise to make the spouse a partner, employee, or member of the board of the corporation. Often, seminars will offer special activities for husbands and wives that will provide documentation later on.

As a general rule, the business deductions are allowed for conventions and seminars held in North America. The IRS is taking a closer look at cruise-ship seminars and is now requiring two statements to be attached to the tax return. The first statement substantiates the number of days on the ship, the number of hours spent each day on business, and the activities in the program. The second statement must come from the sponsor of the convention to verify the first information. In addition, the ship must be registered in the United States, and all ports of call must be located in the United States or its possessions. Again, the key for the taxpayer taking this sort of deduction is careful documentation and substantiation.

What Goes into a Logbook

Keeping a logbook or expense diary is probably the best line of defense for the business person with respect to business expenses incurred while traveling. If you are on the road, keep these things in mind:

With respect to travel expenses:

Keep proof of the costs,

Record the time of departure,

Record the number of days spent on business,

List the places visited and the business purposes of your activities.

With respect to the transportation costs:

Keep copies of all receipts in excess of $25, and if traveling by car keep track of mileage; and

Log all other expenses in your diary.

Similarly, with meals, tips, and lodging, keep receipts for all items over $25 and make sure to record all less-expensive items in your logbook.

Business persons may also take tax deductions for their attendance at workshops, seminars, retreats, and the like, provided they are careful to document the business nature of the trip. Accurate recordkeeping is the first line of defense for tax preparation. Note that it is no longer possible to deduct for investment seminars or conventions, as opposed to business conventions.

Charitable Deductions

The law provides that an individual or business can donate either money or property to qualified charities and take a tax deduction for the donation. Individuals are afforded more favorable deductions for donations of money or property they own than are artists donating their own creations or business people who donate property out of their inventory. Since this area can be quite technical, you should consult with your tax advisor before making any charitable donations. In addition, there have been some abuses on the part of charities which resulted in misappropriations of donated funds. If you have any question about the validity of a particular charity, you should contact your state attorney general's office or the local governmental agency which polices charitable solicitations in your area.

Grants, Prizes, and Awards

Individuals who receive income from grants or fellowships should be aware that this income can be excluded from gross income and thus represents considerable tax savings. To qualify for this exclusion the grant must be for the purpose of furthering one's education and training. However, amounts received under a grant or fellowship that are specifically designated to cover expenses related to the grant are no longer fully deductible. Furthermore, if the grant is given as compensation for services or is primarily for the benefit of the grant-giving organization, it cannot be excluded.

For scholarships and fellowships granted after August 16, 1986, the deduction is allowed only if the recipient is a degree candidate. The amount of the exclusion from income is limited to the amounts used for tuition, fees, books, supplies, and equipment. Amounts designated for room, board, and other incidental expenses are included in income. No exclusion from income is allowed for recipients who are not degree candidates.

The above rules apply to income from grants and fellowships. Unfortunately, the Tax Reform Act of 1986 also put tighter restrictions on money, goods, or services received as prizes or awards. Previously, the amounts received for certain awards were excluded from income, if the recipient was rewarded for past achievements and had not applied for the award. Examples of this type of award are the Pulitzer Prize or the Nobel Prize. Under the present law, any prizes or awards for religious, charitable, scientific, or artistic achievements are included as income to the recipient unless the prize is assigned to charity.

If you do not know whether a particular activity is deductible, you should consult with a competent CPA or tax advisor before embarking on it. In any case, consultation with competent tax professionals is always advisable to ensure maximum benefits.

20

Are You Zoned to Work at Home?

It is common for the small-business owner to have an office or workshop in a home or garage. The problems raised by the multiple use of a dwelling can be divided into two basic areas: whether local zoning regulations legally allow working and living in the same place, and whether the income tax laws recognize the realities of business start-ups. For a full discussion of the income tax considerations of designating a part of your home as an office, see "Deductions for the Use of a Home in Business," page 157. In this chapter I will discuss the zoning problem.

Local Zoning Restrictions

For the person who wants to live and work in the same space, local zoning ordinances can be a significant hindrance. Some city and country ordinances flatly prohibit using the same space as a business and as a dwelling. In some commercially zoned areas where low-cost lofts and studios are available, it is illegal to maintain a residence in the same space. In residential areas, regulations may require permits and restrict the size and use of the work space.

Municipal and county ordinances vary, and the business owner should, therefore, check with the appropriate local government agency to determine specific requirements. The fire department, for example, would undoubtedly have to approve the use of a kiln.

For the person who wants to maintain an office or workshop in the garage or basement of a residence, several types of restrictions may apply. The space devoted to the work activity may be limited to a certain number of square feet; outbuildings may or may not be allowed. The type of equipment used may also be restricted. Noise, smoke, and odor restrictions may apply, and approval may be required from all or some of the neighbors. If remodeling is contemplated, building codes must, of course, also be considered.

You also may have to obtain a home-occupation permit or, in many areas, a business license. The application fee for either of these will normally be a flat fee or a percentage of annual receipts from the activity. Depending upon the success of the business, this could become a substantial expense. In addition, your homeowner's or renter's insurance policy may contain some restrictions relating to commercial activity. You should contact your insurance broker to find out whether your policy contains such limitations and what can be done to deal with them.

In commercially zoned areas, small manufacturers may have more flexibility in the types of activities they conduct, particularly if they produce noise or odors that would be offensive to others in a residentially zoned location. But if you also wish to use the work space for eating and sleeping, zoning ordinances may prohibit such use.

Some cities have recognized the hardships these zoning ordinances create for artists and craftspeople. In New York City, a municipal dwelling law was enacted exempting artists and their families from restrictions against living and working in the same apartment unit. The state of California also enacted legislation that grants local municipalities the right to adopt zoning ordinances that would accommodate artists who live in industrially or commercially zoned areas.

While these laws have solved the immediate problem of artists and craftspeople living and working in the same location, new problems have been created. Once it became possible for artists to live and work in the Soho district of New York City, for example, the area became a magnet for galleries, boutiques, restaurants, and tourists. Many artists remain, but many others have been forced out by skyrocketing rents and prices. Before Soho became fashionable, no new industry could be enticed into the area. Consequently, landlords were pleased to have artists leasing their commercial property. Once development caught on, however, buildings changed hands more often, and artists and craftspeople who had invested substantial sums in their lofts found that their commercial leases afforded them little protection.

However, a 1979 New York case, *Mandel* v. *Pitkowsky*, may provide residential loft tenants with some degree of security. Pitkowsky and sculptor Ulrich Niemeyer rented commercial quarters for ten years. Their lease limited their occupancy to an artist's studio. Nevertheless, their landlord encouraged them to convert the studio into their residence. Both sides were happy to abide by this illegal arrangement, apparently secure in the knowledge that the city was not diligently inspecting these properties.

When the lease expired, the landlord demanded a threefold increase in the rent. The landlord claimed that because the property was commercial rather than residential, it was not subject to the city's rent-stabilization laws. The court did not agree; the landlord's express approval of the tenants' ten-year residency converted the studio into a de facto multiple dwelling for purposes of the rent-stabilization laws.

Federal Regulations

Another type of regulation that can adversely affect those who want to work at home are federal laws that inhibit cottage industries. The U.S. Department of Labor is actively enforcing a 1943 regulation that forbids individuals from producing in their homes for profit the following six categories of goods: embroidery, women's apparel, gloves and mittens, buttons and buckles, jewelry, and handkerchiefs.

The regulation was originally enacted many years ago when the Department of Labor found that minimum-wage violations were widespread in industries in which working at home predominated. The minimum wage is mandated by the federal Fair Labor Standards Act, and requires employers to pay their employees no less than a set hourly rate. Overtime, at one-and-one-half times the employees' hourly rate, is also mandated for hours worked over forty hours per week.

In 1981, the department proposed repealing all regulations that prohibited cottage industries, but bitter labor union opposition resulted in the continuation of the regulation for all the targeted crafts except knitted outerwear, and even that exemption is still being considered in the courts.

The remaining regulations may create serious difficulties for people who want to work at home. In recent years, the disputes between labor unions, principally the International Ladies Garment Workers Union, and women who make their living from cottage industries has become quite heated. The unions argue that they merely want to prevent sweatshop conditions, but many people believe that the real issue is non-unionized home labor competing with union members who work in unionized factories.

In order to fall within the scope of the regulation, the worker must be an employee. This does not mean, however, that a person can avoid the effect of the regulation simply by labeling himself or herself an independent contractor. Under the Fair Labor Standards Act, the test of employment is the economic reality of the relationship.

For example, the Supreme Court has held that members of a cooperative are employees for the purposes of the home-worker regulation. The decision was based on several factors including the fact that the cooperative's management decides the work to be performed and who is to do it. The management also decides who can become a member of the cooperative, and can terminate the relationship if a member's work is substandard.

At the other end of the spectrum are manufacturers who are self-employed and independent, selling their products on the open market, at wholesale or retail, for whatever price they can command. In this situation, the federal regulations do not apply. But for some people, the 1943 regulation poses a serious difficulty in living and working at home.

21

Renting Commercial Space

At some point in the life of your business, you will probably find it necessary to evaluate the terms and conditions of a commercial lease. These are much more subject to negotiation and pitfalls than residential leases, which are more tightly regulated in most states. You should consult an attorney with experience in negotiating commercial leases before signing one. This discussion is intended to alert you to some of the topics which should arise in your discussion with your lawyer.

To begin with, the exact space to be rented should be spelled out in the lease, in detail. If your space is in a shopping center and you share responsibility for common areas with other tenants, these responsibilities should be explained. Will you be responsible for cleaning and maintaining them, or will the landlord? When will the common areas be open or closed? What other facilities are available to you, such as restrooms, storage, and the like?

Another important item is the cost of the space. Will you be paying a flat monthly rental or one which will change based on your earnings at the location, as is often the case when stores lease space in a shopping center? In order to evaluate the cost of the space, you should compare it with other similar spaces in the same locale. Do not be afraid to negotiate for more favorable terms. Care should be taken not to sign a lease which will restrict you from opening another facility close to the one being rented.

It is also important for you to consider the period of the lease. If, for example, you are merely renting a booth at a trade show, then you are only concerned with a short term. On the other hand, if you intend to rent for a year or two, it is a good idea to get an option to extend because when you advertise and promote your business, your location is one of the things you will be telling people about. Moving can cause a lot of problems with mail and telephone numbers. Besides, if you move every year or two, some customers may feel that you are unstable, and customers who buy on an irregular basis may not know where to find you after the lease period ends. Worse still, they may find a competitor in your old space.

Long-term leases are recordable in some states. Recording, where permitted, is generally accomplished by having the lease filed in the same office as a deed to the property would be filed. Check with a local real estate title company or real estate attorney for the particulars in your state. If you are in a position to record your lease, it is probably a good idea to do so since you will then be entitled to receive legal and other notices which are related to the property.

It is essential for you to determine whether there are any restrictions on the particular activity you wish to perform on the leased premises. For example, the area may be zoned so as to prohibit you from manufacturing. It is a good idea to insist on a provision which puts the burden of obtaining any permit or variances on the landlord or, if you are responsible for them, the inability to obtain them should be grounds for terminating the lease without penalty.

Be sure the lease provides that you are permitted to use any sign or advertising on the premises, or spells out any restrictions. It is not uncommon, for example, for historic landmark laws to regulate signs on old buildings. Can you put a sign in your window or in front of your building? Some zoning laws prohibit this.

You should also be aware that extensive remodeling may be necessary for certain spaces to become suitable for your use. If this is the case then it is important for you to determine who will be responsible for the costs of remodeling. In addition, it is essential to find out whether it will be necessary for you to restore the premises to their original, pre-remodeled condition when the lease ends. This can be expensive and, in some instances, impossible.

Who Pays for What?

If you need special hook-ups, such as water or electrical lines, you should determine whether the landlord will provide them or whether you have to bear the cost. Of course, if the leased premises already have the necessary facilities, you should question the landlord regarding the cost of these utilities. Are they included in the rent or are they to be paid separately?

In some locations, garbage pick-up is not a problem, since it is one of the services provided by the municipality. On the other hand, it is common for renters to be responsible for their own trash disposal. In commercial spaces, this can be quite expensive and should be addressed in the lease.

Customarily, the landlord will be responsible for the exterior of the building. It will be the landlord's obligation to make sure that it does not leak during rainstorms and that it is properly ventilated. Notwithstanding this fact, it is important for you to make sure the lease deals with the question of responsibility if, for example, the building is damaged and some of your work or equipment is damaged or destroyed. Will you have to take out insurance for the building as well as its contents, or will the landlord assume responsibility for the building insurance?

Similarly, you should find out whether it will be your obligation to obtain liability insurance for injuries which are caused in portions of the building not under your control, such as common hallways and stair wells. You should, of course, have your own liability policy for accidental injuries or accidents which occur on your leased premises.

Security and Zoning

A good lease will also contain a provision dealing with security. If you are renting indoor space in a shopping center, it is likely that the landlord will be responsible for external security, although this is not universally the case. If you are renting an entire building, it is customarily your responsibility to provide whatever security you deem important. Does the lease permit you to install locks or alarm systems? If this is something you are interested in, you should address the question.

Does the lease have any restrictions on deliveries, their time, or location? If you are dealing with large bulky items and are accepting deliveries or making them, your lease should contain a provision which will give you the flexibility you desire.

If the place you wish to rent will be used as both your personal dwelling and for business, other problems may arise. It is quite common for zoning laws to prohibit certain forms of commercial activities when the area is zoned residential (see Chapter 20). You should consult with your attorney before attempting to operate out of your home.

Finally, it is essential for you to be sure that every item agreed upon between you and the landlord is stated in writing. This is particularly important when dealing with leases since many state laws provide that a long-term lease is an interest in land and can only be enforced if in writing.

The relationship between landlords and tenants is an ancient one which is undergoing a good deal of change. Care should be taken when examining a potential business location to determine exactly what you can do on the premises and whether the landlord or municipal rules will allow you to use the location for its intended purpose.

22

Estate Planning

Proper estate planning will require the assistance of a knowledge-able lawyer and perhaps also a life insurance agent, an accountant, or a bank trust officer, depending on the nature and size of the estate. In this chapter we will consider the basic principles of estate planning. This discussion is not a substitute for the aid of a lawyer experienced in estate planning; rather, it is intended to introduce you to the basic principles, alert you to potential problems, and aid in preparing you to work with your estate planner(s).

The Will

A will is a legal instrument by which a person directs the distribu-tion of property in the estate upon death. The maker of the will is called the *testator*. Gifts given by a will are referred to as *bequests* (personal property) or *devises* (real estate). Certain formalities are required by state law to create a valid will. About thirty states allow *only* formally witnessed wills; they require that the instrument be in writing and signed by the testator, in the presence of two or more witnesses. The other half of the states allow *either* witnessed or un-witnessed wills. If a will is entirely hand-written and signed by the testator, it is known as a holographic will.

A will is a unique document in two respects. First, if properly drafted it is *ambulatory*, meaning it can accommodate change, such as applying to property acquired after the will is made. Second, a will is *revocable*, meaning that the testator has the power to change or cancel it before death. Even if a testator makes a valid agreement not to revoke the will, the power to revoke it remains, though liability for breach of contract could result.

Generally, courts do not consider a will to have been revoked unless it can be established that the testator either (1) performed a physical act of revocation, such as burning or tearing up a will, with intent to revoke it; or (2) executed a valid later will which revoked the previous will. Most state statutes also provide for automatic revocation of a will in whole or in part if the testator is subsequently divorced or married.

To change a will, the testator must execute a supplement, known as a *codicil*, which has the same formal requirements as those for creating a will. To the extent that the codicil contradicts the will, those contradicted parts of the will are revoked.

Payment of Testator's Debts

When the property owned by the testator at death is insufficient to satisfy all the bequests in the will after all debts and taxes have been paid, some or all of the bequests in the will must be reduced or even eliminated entirely. The process of reducing or eliminating bequests is known as *abatement*, and the priorities for reduction are set according to the category of each bequest. The legally significant categories of gifts are generally as follows: *specific* bequests or devises, meaning gifts of identifiable items ("I give to X all the furniture in my home"); *demonstrative* bequests or devises, meaning gifts which are to be paid out of a specified source unless that source contains insufficient funds, in which case the gifts will be paid out of the general assets ("I give to Y $1,000 to be paid from my shares of stock in ABC Corporation"); *general* bequests, meaning gifts payable out of the general assets of an estate ("I give Z $1,000"); and finally, *residuary* bequests or devises, or gifts of whatever is left in the estate after all other gifts and expenses are satisfied ("I give the rest, residue and remainder of my estate to Z").

Intestate property, or property not governed by a will, is usually the first to be taken to satisfy claims against the estate. (If the will contains a valid residuary clause, there will be no such property.) Next, residuary bequests will be taken. If more money is needed, general bequests will be taken, and lastly, specific and demonstrative bequests will be taken together in proportion to their value. Some states provide that all gifts, regardless of type, abate proportionately.

Disposition of Property Not Willed

If the testator acquires more property during the time between signing the will and death, the disposition of such property will also be governed by the will, which, as we have seen, is ambulatory in nature. If such property falls within the description of an existing category in the will ("I give all my stock to X; I give all my real estate to Y"), it will pass along with all similar property. If it does not, and the will contains a valid residuary clause, such after-acquired property will go to the residuary legatees. If there is no such clause which applies to this property, such property will pass outside the will to the persons specified in the state's law of intestate succession.

When a person dies without leaving a valid will, this is known as dying *intestate*. The property of a person who dies intestate is distributed according to the state law of intestate succession, which specifies who is entitled to what parts of the estate. An intestate's surviving spouse will always receive a share, generally at least one-third of the estate. An intestate's surviving children likewise always get a share. If some of the children do not survive the intestate, the grandchildren of the intestate may be entitled to a share by representation. *Representation* is a legal principle which means that if an heir does not survive the intestate, but has a child who does survive, that child will represent the non-surviving heir and receive that parent's share in the estate. In other words, the surviving child stands in the shoes of a dead parent in order to inherit from a grandparent who dies intestate.

If there are no direct descendants surviving, the intestate's surviving spouse will take the entire estate or share it with the intestate's parents. If there is neither a surviving spouse nor any surviving direct descendant of the intestate, the estate will be distributed to the intestate's parents, or if the parents are not surviving, to the intestate's siblings by representation. If there are no surviving persons in any of these categories, the estate will go to surviving grandparents and their direct descendants. In this way the family tree is constantly expanded in search of surviving relatives. If none of the persons specified in the law of intestate succession survive the testator, the intestate's property ultimately goes to the state. This is known as *escheat*. It should be noted that the laws of intestate succession make no provision for friends, in-laws, or stepchildren.

State law will often provide a testator's surviving spouse with certain benefits from the estate even if the spouse is left out of the testator's will. Historically, these benefits were known as *dower*, in the case of a surviving wife, or *curtesy*, in the case of a surviving husband. In place of the old dower and curtesy, modern statutes give the surviving spouse the right to "elect" against the will, and thereby receive a share equal to at least one-fourth of the estate. Here again, state laws vary; in some states, the surviving spouse's elective share is one-third. The historical concepts of dower and curtesy are in large part a result of the law's traditional recognition of an absolute duty on the part of the husband to provide for the wife. Modern laws are perhaps better justified by the notion that most property in a marriage should be shared because the financial success of either partner is due to the efforts of both.

Advantages to Having a Will

Now that we have some background as to what a will is and what happens without one, we can begin to look at some of the benefits of having a will.

A will affords the opportunity to direct distribution of one's property and to set out limitations by making gifts conditional. For example, if an individual wishes to donate certain property to a specific charity, but only if certain conditions are adhered to, a will can make such conditions a prerequisite to the donation.

A will permits the testator to nominate an executor, called a "personal representative" in some states, to watch over the estate. If no executor is named in the will, the court will appoint one. If the testator has an unusual type of property, such as antiques, art, or publishable manuscripts, it is a good idea to appoint joint executors, one with financial expertise and the other with expertise in valuation of antiques, or in art, or with publishing. If joint executors are used, some provision should be made in the will for resolving any deadlock between the two. For example, a neutral third party might be appointed as an arbitrator who is directed to resolve any impasses after hearing both sides. It is also advisable to define the scope of the executor's power by detailed instructions. A lawyer's help will be necessary to set forth all of these important considerations in legally enforceable, unambiguous terms. It is essential in a will to avoid careless language which might be subject to attack by survivors unhappy with the will's provisions. A lawyer's help is also crucial to avoid making bequests which are not legally enforceable because contrary to public policy.

In addition to giving the testator significant posthumous control over division of property, a carefully drafted will can greatly reduce the overall amount of estate tax paid at death. The following information on taxing structures relates to federal estate taxation. State estate taxes often contain similar provisions, but state law must always be consulted for specifics.

The Gross Estate

The first step in evaluating an estate for tax purposes is to determine the so-called "gross estate." The *gross estate* will include all property over which the deceased had significant control at the time of death. Examples would include certain life insurance proceeds and annuities, jointly-held interests, and revocable transfers.

Under current tax laws, the executor of an estate may elect to value the property in the estate either as of the date of death or as of a date six months after death. The estate property must be valued in its entirety at the time chosen. However, if the executor elects to value the estate six months after death and certain pieces of property are distributed or sold before then, that property will be valued as of the date of distribution or sale.

Fair market value is defined as the price at which property would change hands between a willing buyer and a willing seller, when both buyer and seller have reasonable knowledge of all relevant facts. Such a determination is often very difficult to make, especially when items such as artwork are involved. Although the initial determination of fair market value is generally made by the executor when the estate tax return is filed, the Internal Revenue Service may disagree with the executor's valuation and assign assets a much higher fair market value. For example, in 1979 the IRS claimed that Jacqueline Susann's diary had an estate tax value of $3,800,000 as a literary property. The diary, which neither Susann nor her executor had considered particularly valuable, had been destroyed by the executor pursuant to Susann's directions.

When an executor and the Internal Revenue Service disagree as to valuation, the court will decide the matter. In most cases, the burden will be on the taxpayer to prove the value of the asset. Thus, expert testimony and evidence of the sale of the same or similar properties will be helpful, as in cases involving original manuscripts and drawings. In general, courts are reluctant to determine valuation by formula.

Generally, estate taxes must be paid when the estate tax return is filed (within nine months of the date of death) although arrangements may be made to spread payments out over a number of years if necessary. It is not uncommon for executors to be forced to sell properties for less than full value in order to pay taxes. This can be avoided by obtaining insurance policies, the proceeds of which can be set up in a trust. (For an explanation of a trust, see the section "Distributing Property Outside the Will," below.)

The law allows a number of deductions from the gross estate in determining the amount of the taxable estate. The taxable estate is the basis upon which the tax owing is computed. The following section gives you a closer look at some of the key deductions used to arrive at the amount of your taxable estate.

The Taxable Estate

Figuring the taxable estate is the second major step in evaluating an estate for tax purposes, after determining the gross estate. Typical deductions from the gross estate include funeral expenses; certain estate administration expenses; debts and enforceable claims against the estate; mortgages and liens; and, perhaps most significant, the marital deduction and the charitable deduction.

The marital deduction allows the total value of any interest in property which passes from the decedent to the surviving spouse to be subtracted from the value of the gross estate. The government will eventually get its tax on this property, when the spouse dies, but only to the extent such interest is included in the spouse's gross estate. This deduction may occur even in the absence of a will making a gift to the surviving spouse, since state law generally provides that the spouse is entitled to at least one-fourth of the overall estate regardless of the provisions of the will.

The charitable deduction refers to the tax deduction allowed upon the transfer of property from an estate to a recognized charity. Since the definition of a charity for tax purposes is quite technical, it is advisable to insert a clause in the will which provides that if the institution specified to receive the donation does not qualify for the charitable deduction, the bequest shall go to a substitute qualified institution at the choice of the executor.

Once deductions are figured, the taxable estate is taxed at the rate specified by the Unified Estate and Gift Tax Schedule. The unified tax imposes the same rate of tax on gifts made by will as on gifts made during life. It is a progressive tax, meaning the percent paid in taxes increases with the amount of property involved. The rates rise significantly for larger estates, for example, from 18 percent where the cumulative total of taxable estate and taxable gifts is under $10,000, to 55 percent where the cumulative total is over $3,000,000. Tax credits are provided by year according to the tax schedule. Federal estate tax is also reduced by state death tax credit or actual state death tax, whichever is less. Tax credits result in a $600,000 exemption, which is available to every estate. This exemption, combined with the unlimited marital deduction, allows most estates to escape estate taxes altogether.

Distributing Property Outside the Will

Property can be distributed outside of the will by making *intervivos* gifts (given during the giver's lifetime) either outright or by placing the property in trust prior to death. The main advantage to distributing property outside of the will is that the property escapes the delays and expense of probate, the court procedure by which a will is validated and administered. It used to be that there were also significant tax advantages to making intervivos gifts rather than gifts by will, but since the estate and gift-tax rates are now unified, there are few remaining tax advantages. One remaining advantage to making an intervivos gift is that if the gift appreciates in value between the time the gift is made and death, the appreciated value will not be taxed. If the gift were made by will, the added value would be taxable since the gift would be valued as of date of death (or six months after). This value difference can represent significant tax savings for the heirs of someone whose business suddenly becomes successful and rapidly increases in value.

The other advantage to making an intervivos gift involves the yearly exclusion. A yearly exclusion of $10,000 per recipient is available on intervivos gifts. For example, if $15,000 worth of gifts were given to an individual in one year, only $5,000 worth of gifts will actually be taxable to the donor (who is responsible for the gift tax). A married couple can combine their gifts and claim a yearly exclusion of $20,000 per recipient. Gifts made within three years of death used to be included in the gross estate on the theory that they were made in contemplation of death. Recent amendments to the tax laws, however, have done away with the three-year rule for most purposes. The three-year rule is still applicable to gifts of life insurance and to certain transfers involving stock redemptions or tax liens; the rule also applies to certain valuation schemes, the details of which are too complex to discuss here.

Gift-tax returns must be filed by the donor for any year where gifts made exceeded $10,000 to any one donee. It is not necessary to file returns when a gift to any one donee amounts to less than $10,000. However, where it is possible that valuation of the gift will become an issue with the IRS, it may be a good idea to file a return anyway. Filing the return starts the three-year statute of limitations running. Once the statute of limitations period has expired, the IRS will be barred from filing suit for unpaid taxes or for tax deficiencies due to higher government valuations of the gifts. If a taxpayer omits includable gifts amounting to more than 25 percent of the total amount of gifts stated in the return, the statute of limitations is extended to six years. There is no statute of limitations for fraudulent returns filed with the intent to evade tax.

In order to qualify as an intervivos, or living, gift for tax purposes, a gift must be complete and final. Control is an important issue. If a giver retains the right to revoke a gift, the gift may be found to be testamentary in nature, even if the right to revoke was never exercised (unless the gift was made in trust). The gift must also be delivered. An actual, physical delivery is best, but a symbolic delivery may suffice if there is strong evidence of intent to make an irrevocable gift. An example of symbolic delivery is when the donor puts something in a safe and gives the intended recipient the only key.

Another common way to transfer property outside the will is to place the property in a trust which is created prior to death. A *trust* is simply a legal arrangement by which one person holds certain property for the benefit of another. The person holding the property is the *trustee*; those for whose benefit it is held are the *beneficiaries*. To create a valid trust, the giver must identify the trust property;

make a declaration of intent to create the trust; transfer property to the trust; and name identifiable beneficiaries. If no trustee is named, a court will appoint one. The settlor, or creator of the trust, may also be designated as trustee, in which case segregation of the trust property satisfies the delivery requirement. Trusts can be created by will, in which case they are termed testamentary trusts, but these trust properties will be probated along with the rest of the will. To avoid probate, the settlor must create a valid intervivos trust—one given while the giver is alive.

Generally, in order to qualify as an intervivos trust, a valid interest in property must be transferred before the death of the creator of the trust. If the settlor fails to name a beneficiary for the trust or make delivery of the property to the trustee before death, the trust will likely be termed testamentary. Such a trust will be deemed invalid unless the formalities required for creating a will were complied with.

A trust will not be termed testamentary simply because the settlor retained significant control over the trust, such as the power to revoke or modify the trust. For example, when a person makes a deposit in a savings account in his or her own name as trustee for another, and reserves the power to withdraw the money or revoke the trust, the trust will be enforceable by the beneficiary upon the death of the depositor, providing the depositor has not in fact revoked the trust. Many states allow the same type of arrangement in authorizing joint bank accounts with rights of survivorship as valid will substitutes. Property transferred under one of these arrangements is thus passed outside the will and need not go through probate. However, even though such an arrangement escapes probate, the trust property will probably be counted as part of the gross estate for tax purposes because the settlor retained significant control. In addition, if the deceased settlor created a revocable trust for the purpose of decreasing the share of a surviving spouse, in some states the trust will be declared illusory—in effect invalid. The surviving spouse is then granted the legal share not only from the probated estate but from the revocable trust.

Life insurance trusts can be used for paying estate taxes. The proceeds will not be taxed if the life insurance trust is irrevocable and the beneficiary is someone other than the estate, such as a friend or relative in an individual capacity or the business. This is especially important for entrepreneurs, since without a life insurance trust their survivors might be forced to sell estate assets for less than their real value in order to pay estate taxes.

Conclusion

All business persons should give some thought to estate planning and take the time to execute a will. Without a will, there is simply no way to control the disposition of one's property. Sound estate planning may include transfers outside of the will since these types of arrangements escape the delays and expenses of probate. Certain types of trusts can be valuable will substitutes, but they may be subject to challenge by a surviving spouse. Since successful estate planning is complex, it is essential to work with a lawyer skilled in this field.

23

How to Find a Lawyer and Accountant

Most business people expect to seek the advice of a lawyer only occasionally, for counseling on important matters such as the decision to incorporate or the purchase of a building. If this is your concept of the attorney's role in your business, I recommend you re-evaluate it. Most small businesses would operate more efficiently and more profitably in the long run if they had a relationship with a business attorney more like that between a family doctor and his patient, i.e., an ongoing relationship which allows the attorney to get to know the business well enough to engage in preventative legal counseling and assist in planning, thus making possible the solution of many problems before they occur.

If your business is small now or undercapitalized, you are doubt-less anxious to keep operating costs down. You probably do not relish the idea of paying an attorney to get to know your business if you are not involved in an immediate crisis. However, it is a good bet that a visit with a competent business lawyer right now will result in the raising of issues vital to the future of your business. There is good reason why larger, successful businesses employ one or more attorneys full time as in-house counsel. Ready access to legal advice is something you should not deny your business at any time, for any reason.

An attorney experienced in business law can give you important information regarding the risks unique to your business. Further-more, the lawyer can advise you regarding your rights and obligations in your relationship with present and future employees, the rules that apply in your state regarding the hiring and firing of employees, permissible collection practices, and so forth. Ignorance of these issues and violation of the rules can result in financially devastating lawsuits and even criminal penalties. Each state has its own laws covering certain business practices; thus state laws must be consulted on many areas covered in this book. A competent local business attorney is, therefore, your best source of information on many issues which will arise in the running of your business.

What is really behind all the hoopla about preventive legal counseling? Are we lawyers simply seeking more work? Admittedly, as business people, lawyers want business. But what you should consider is economic reality: *Most legal problems cost more to solve or defend than it would have cost to prevent their occurrence in the first place.* Litigation is notoriously inefficient and expensive. You do not want to sue or to be sued, if you can help it. The expense is shocking; for instance, it can cost close to $100 per day simply to use a courtroom for trial. Pretrial procedures run into the thousands of dollars on most cases. The cost of defending a case filed against you or your business is something you have no choice but to incur, unless you choose to default, which is almost never advisable.

The lawyer who will be most valuable to your young business will likely not be a Raymond Burr or Robert Redford character, but rather a meticulous person who does most of his or her work in an office, going over your business forms, your employee contracts, or your corporate bylaws. This person should have a good reputation in the legal community, as well as the business community. You might pay $100 per hour for the attorney, but if the firm has a good reputation, it likely employs a well-trained professional staff which can reduce the amount of attorney time required.

One of the first items you should discuss with your lawyer is the fee structure. You are entitled to an estimate, though unless you enter into an agreement to the contrary with the attorney, the estimate is just that. Business lawyers generally charge by the hour, though you may be quoted a flat rate for a specific service such as incorporation or registering your trademark.

Finding a Lawyer

If you do not know any attorneys, ask other business people whether they know any good ones. You want either a lawyer who specializes in business, or a general practitioner who has many happy business clients. Finding the lawyer who is right for you is like finding the right doctor; you may have to shop around a bit. Your city, county, and state bar associations may have helpful referral services. A good tip is to find out who is in the business law section of the state or county bar association, or who has served on special bar committees dealing with law reform. It may also be useful to find out whether any articles covering the area of law you are concerned with have been published in either scholarly journals or continuing-legal-education publications, and if the author is available to assist you. It is a good idea to hire a specialist or law firm with a number of specialists rather than a general practitioner. While it is true that you may pay more per hour for the expert, still, you will not have to fund his learning time, and experience is valuable. In this regard, you may wish to keep in mind that it is uncommon for a lawyer to specialize in business practice and also handle criminal matters. Thus, if you are faced with a criminal prosecution for the death of an employee as discussed in Chapter 16, then you should be searching for an experienced criminal defense lawyer.

One method by which you can attempt to evaluate an attorney in regard to representing business clients is by consulting the *Martindale-Hubbell Law Directory* in your local county law library. While this may be useful, the mere fact that an attorney's name does not appear in the book should not be given too much weight, since there is a charge for being included and some lawyers may have chosen not to pay for the listing.

After you have been given or obtained several recommendations about attorneys, it is appropriate for you to talk with them for a short period of time to determine whether you would be comfortable working with them. Do not be afraid to ask about their background experience, and whether they feel they can help you.

Once you have completed the interview process, select the person who appears to satisfy your needs. The rest is up to you. Contact your lawyer whenever you believe a legal question has arisen. Your attorney should aid you in identifying which questions require legal action or advice and which require business decisions. Generally, lawyers will deal only with legal issues, though they may help you to evaluate business problems.

I encourage my clients to feel comfortable about calling me at the office during the day or at home in the evening. Some lawyers, however, may resent having their personal time invaded. Some, in fact, do not list their home telephone number. You should learn your attorney's preference early on.

The attorney-client relationship is such that you should feel comfortable when confiding in your attorney. This person will not disclose your confidential communications; in fact, a violation of this rule, depending on the circumstances, can be considered an ethical breach which could subject the attorney to professional sanctions.

If you take the time to develop a good working relationship with your attorney it may well prove to be one of your more valuable business assets.

Finding an Accountant

In addition to an attorney, most small businesses will need the services of a competent accountant to aid with tax planning and the filing of periodic and annual tax returns. Finding a CPA with whom your business is compatible is similar to finding an attorney. You should ask around and learn which accountants are servicing businesses similar to yours. State professional accounting associations may also provide a referral service or point you to a directory of accountants in your region. You should interview prospective accountants to determine whether you feel you can work with them and whether you feel their skill will be compatible with your business needs.

Like your attorney, your accountant can provide valuable assistance in planning for the future of your business. It is important to work with professionals you trust and with whom you are able to relate on a professional level.

Index

If not available at your
local bookstore, this book may
be ordered by sending $8.95
plus one dollar for postage and handling
to the address below.

Madrona Publishers
Department X, P. O. Box 22667
Seattle, WA 98122

Prepaid orders only, please.
Add one dollar for postage and handling
for the first book and
fifty cents for each additional book.

Mastercharge and Visa cardholders
may order by calling (206) 325-3973.